S. Hrg. 113–677

DISMANTLING IRAN'S NUCLEAR WEAPONS PROGRAM: NEXT STEPS TO ACHIEVE A COMPREHENSIVE DEAL

HEARING

BEFORE THE

COMMITTEE ON FOREIGN RELATIONS UNITED STATES SENATE

ONE HUNDRED THIRTEENTH CONGRESS

SECOND SESSION

DECEMBER 3, 2014

Printed for the use of the Committee on Foreign Relations

Available via the World Wide Web: http://www.gpo.gov/fdsys/

U.S. GOVERNMENT PUBLISHING OFFICE

95–460 PDF   WASHINGTON : 2015

For sale by the Superintendent of Documents, U.S. Government Publishing Office
Internet: bookstore.gpo.gov   Phone: toll free (866) 512–1800; DC area (202) 512–1800
Fax: (202) 512–2104   Mail: Stop IDCC, Washington, DC 20402–0001

(II)

CONTENTS

DISMANTLING IRAN'S NUCLEAR WEAPONS PROGRAM: NEXT STEPS TO ACHIEVE A COMPREHENSIVE DEAL

WEDNESDAY, DECEMBER 3, 2014

U.S. SENATE,
COMMITTEE ON FOREIGN RELATIONS,
Washington, DC.

The committee met, pursuant to notice, at 1:45 p.m, in room SD–419, Dirksen Senate Office Building, Hon. Robert Menendez (chairman of the committee) presiding.

Present: Senators Menendez, Murphy, Kaine, Markey, Corker, Risch, Johnson, Flake, Barrasso, and Paul.

OPENING STATEMENT OF HON. ROBERT MENENDEZ, U.S. SENATOR FROM NEW JERSEY

The CHAIRMAN. This hearing will come to order.

First of all, let me apologize to my colleagues as well as to our panelists. We are still dealing with the aftermath of Superstorm Sandy in New Jersey and in the New Jersey-New York region, and we had the Administrator of FEMA in a meeting on some of the critical issues that seem still not to be resolved. So it just got extended a little longer than I thought. So I apologize to everybody.

Today we have an expert panel to provide an assessment of the status of the P5+1[1] talks and the likelihood of reaching a complete political framework for a comprehensive deal in the next 4 months. I am particularly interested in your views on whether reaching a deal is simply a matter of time or if there has been a fundamental shift in Iranian thinking that makes a deal 4 months from now more likely than in the past 12.

While I believe the administration's diplomatic efforts to terminate Iran's illicit nuclear program should be commended, I am concerned that Iran has not demonstrated a sincere interest in reaching agreement and has used these talks to chip away at our positions, beginning with the concessions on enrichment in the Joint Plan of Action.

Given continued Iranian intransigence in the talks, the failure to conclude a final deal by November 24 falls squarely on Iran. Yet, for over 1 year, we remain trapped in the same fruitless, cyclical narrative which has us conceding our positions, transforming the Arak reactor rather than dismantling it, converting Fordow for some alternate use rather than closing it, and disconnecting cen-

---

[1] [The P5+1 is made up of the five permanent members of the United Nations Security Council (China, France, Russia, the United Kingdom, and the United States), plus Germany.]

(1)

trifuges rather than destroying them. And perhaps more significantly, Iran is not budging on full access to questionable sites and the duration of the agreement.

I understand that the P5+1 members want to put a year on the breakout clock, but I am not convinced a year is enough if we leave the majority of Iran's nuclear infrastructure in place and give up the only leverage we have by providing sanctions relief. The 1-year alarm will give us time to respond, but our only option at that point will likely be a military option. In my view, to suggest that we can quickly or easily rebuild the sanctions regime or replicate the economic pressure currently facing Iran is a false narrative.

For me, this equation is simple. Iran must make up its mind about what is more important: its nuclear weapons program or the welfare of its people. And clearly for the last year, Iran has not felt a need to make that decision.

Right now, we are playing right into the Iranian narrative. So while they have maximized their demands at the negotiating table, we seemed to have minimized ours with no consequences. This is a worst case scenario. It is extremely dangerous for global nonproliferation imperatives and for regional stability and could leave Iran as a nuclear threshold state.

At the end of the day, if no deal is reached by March 24, congressional action to authorize prospective sanctions may provide the leverage we need to prevent Iran from becoming a nuclear weapons state.

Iran's nuclear weapons ambitions and its continued obfuscation at the negotiating table have raised alarms throughout the Middle East and the international community. The risk of a nuclear arms race in the region is not hypothetical. We are seeing the repercussions of permitting Iran to retain an enrichment program resonate in the region, and in our 1–2–3 negotiations with other countries who are asking why they need to accept a no-enrichment standard when Iran will be allowed to enrich.

For me, the time has come to ask whether repeated negotiation extensions, coupled with sanctions relief in the billions of dollars, will ever result in a comprehensive deal. Iran benefits from successive rounds of unfreezing of assets abroad and has not felt the need to make any real concessions beyond the requirements of the interim agreement.

The assumption seems to be that another extension will result in a good deal, and all we have to do is continue negotiating, putting more time on the nuclear breakout clock. My own perspective is that more time will not make a difference on this. The Ayatollah has come to the fundamental decisions that are essential for being able to strike such a deal. Tehran's desire for a nuclear program has not changed, and it is unlikely to change in my view under the present set of circumstances. Iran is negotiating because it wants economic relief, and it is betting that more time on the clock benefits its position.

I know that there are those who suggest that, well, we really have not lifted the sanctions. The sanctions regime is largely in place. Well, the Iranian economy is rebounding. There is greater confidence. There is also a view, I think, that the Iranians have that there is no credible use of force threat on the table. And if you keep coming toward my position in a negotiation as I sit there, then I want to sit there as long as I can because it keeps looking better and better to me. And that is my sense of where we are at today. To hear that we have some significant progress, I do not understand why it takes 7 months if we are on the threshold of making decisions that can be an acceptable deal to be brought to the United States and the international community.

So what I would like to hear from the witnesses as specifically and directly as possible is how we change the environment surrounding the talks and have a set of circumstances and conditions in which Iran is felt compelled to get to a final deal.

The bottom line is from my perspective I continue to believe that we have leverage in this negotiation but leverage that is unused is leverage that is meaningless.

With that, I would like to recognize the distinguished ranking member for his comments, Senator Corker.

STATEMENT OF HON. BOB CORKER, U.S. SENATOR FROM TENNESSEE

Senator CORKER. Well, thank you, Mr. Chairman. I appreciate you calling this timely hearing.

I want to thank the witnesses for being here. I know we have worked around some logistical issues, and it looks like it worked out perfectly actually.

I would also like to say that I know that we are going to have a hearing tomorrow, a little meeting tomorrow afternoon, a smaller meeting. But we still do not have any language at all relative to what this extension even says. I think most of it probably is like it has been, but we really do not have any insight into that. And so, where we are is what many of us were concerned about on the front end, and that is it looks like we may end up with a series of rolling extensions.

If you look at the history of all of this—and I think Henry Kissinger does a great job in his latest book really referring to this issue we are talking about today. But the longer Iran waits, things continue to get better and better and better for them. And I know our chairman outlined that today. But I will just say we have gone from turning Arak into a light water reactor—and by the way, this is based on what we understand. Again, we have not really seen anything in writing. But turning Arak into a light water reactor to allowing it to be a modified heavy water reactor, from shuttering Fordow to letting it continue as a research facility, from dismantling centrifuges to unplugging them, and from demanding full disclosure on possible military dimensions of their nuclear program to accepting only transparency at the margins. And when we have the IAEA having difficulty today even getting Iran to comply with information, obviously that gives great concerns. And obviously the issue of just their effect on the region, its effect right now on what we are doing in Syria—all of these things lead one to be very concerned about where we are.

And I know that we are all going to be looking at how we might play a role. I know the chairman has offered some legislation. Others have looked at ways of Congress affecting the outcome here.

But I just want to close with this. As we sit back and think about these negotiations, I think many of us thought we would start with a—we would end up with a 20-year agreement where you had some meaningful length of time that whatever you agreed to would be in place and that we would understand the military dimensions before any agreement was reached—which would allow you to have some insight into the IRGC [Iranian Revolutionary Guard Corps] and what their activities have been—which obviously this agreement is not going to include.

But when you think about it, we are talking double digits. Knowing the administration the way most of us do, that probably means 10 years, the first double digit. Iran is talking 5 years. My guess is as they sit and wait, the administration may be leaning toward a 7- to 8-year agreement. And so when you think about it, all of this, this incredible regime that our chairman and so many of us have worked on to put in place, will be totally dissipated, the way the administration is now going, over to a 7- to 8-year period. They then will be a valid member of the NPT community, a valid member. We will lose the insights into the possible covert dimensions.

And it really does appear we are going to a place where we really are not getting anything. And of course, their strategy is they are hopeful that this will happen and that over time they will be in a place—by the way, we are not dealing with any of the delivery systems in this agreement. So they have the ability during this 7- to 8-year period to continue to develop deliver systems. We are not dealing with that. So from their standpoint, it puts them in a position, when we are not in the same place, to be in a stronger place themselves. Our position is we are hoping—hoping—that somehow there is a difference of viewpoint at the regime level. But when you think about where we are, it is really not a good place.

And so I do hope that we as a committee, I hope that Congress will figure out the appropriate way to give the administration leverage to really strengthen an agreement that already has gone way down a path that I think is very unhealthy for our country.

Mr. Chairman, thank you for this hearing. I look forward to our outstanding private witnesses and to the questions that come after.

The CHAIRMAN. Thank you, Senator Corker.

Just for the record, we did invite the administration to send us a witness for public purposes, and they declined saying that they would only send us a witness in a secured setting. I will say that at the end of the last round and the pursuit of an extension, we had Wendy Sherman here talking about the parameters of that. I do not know what has changed so dramatically that we could not have any public setting, understanding there would be elements of that that would only be appropriate to discuss in a secured setting, that we could not have a broader discussion about what we hope to achieve, what we are trying to achieve, where we are at in very broad terms. But that is the administration's decision. Hence, we are only pursuing today a private but distinguished panel nonetheless. So we appreciate all of you being here.

Let me introduce you. David Albright, the president of the Institute for Science and International Security. Mr. Albright is no stranger to the committee. He has been here several times, and we welcome you back and the insights you provide for us. Dr. Michael

Doran, who is a senior fellow at the Hudson Institute; and Dr. Gary Samore, who is the executive director for research at the Belfer Center for Science and International Affairs at Harvard's Kennedy School.

And with that, I will remind you all that your full statements will be included in the record, without objection. If you can try to summarize in about 5 minutes or so, we would appreciate it so we can enter into a dialogue with you where many of the elements of your statement, I am sure, will be discussed. And with that, we will recognize Mr. Albright first.

STATEMENT OF DAVID ALBRIGHT, PRESIDENT, INSTITUTE FOR SCIENCE AND INTERNATIONAL SECURITY, WASHINGTON, DC

Mr. ALBRIGHT. Mr. Chairman, Ranking Member Corker, and other esteemed Senators, thank you for inviting me again to testify. I view your work here extremely valuable.

Also, this is a very appropriate time to step back and take stock of the efforts to achieve a comprehensive agreement. And I think I should make clear from the beginning, I mean, for people like myself, the main problem, and the reason for the two extensions, is Iran's refusal to make the necessary concessions to obtain a good deal. Many core issues remain unresolved.

Now, as the absence of Wendy Sherman demonstrates, the ongoing negotiations for this deal are highly detailed and secret, and many technical provisions are being studied and proposed. And little of that has been made public.

Despite that limitation, I would like to talk about some things I think can be identified. Some of this will be repetitive. So I apologize for that.

But the primary goal of the comprehensive solution is to ensure that Iran's nuclear program is indeed peaceful against a background of two decades of Iran deceiving the IAEA about its nuclear programs, including military nuclear programs. And this long history of deception and violation places additional burdens on achieving a verifiable, long-term agreement, including the need for any agreement to last for 20 years. I think if you look at the work the IAEA has to do, it is not going to be done after 7 to 10 years. There is a need for an extensive duration for this agreement.

I think it is also accepted that a good deal should increase significantly the time needed to produce enough nuclear explosive material for a nuclear weapon, typically called the breakout timeline. And U.S. officials have talked often about achieving breakout times of 1 year. And to do that, I think we are all aware that significant limitations in the number of centrifuges will have to occur. Iran is going to need to reduce the size of its uranium, natural uranium and low-enriched uranium stocks, and it is going to have to limit its centrifuge R&D program.

Also to get a sound deal, Iran is going to have to verifiably address the IAEA's concerns about Iran's past and possibly ongoing work related to nuclear weapons, and it needs to do that before a deal is signed or any relief from economic or financial sanctions occurs. Now, in the latter case, a deal could be signed but it would be followed by an implementation period, during which Iran would implement its key commitments, including addressing the IAEA's concerns before any key economic or financial sanctions are relaxed.

And of course, the agreement is going to have to include verification provisions that go beyond the additional protocol. And these supplementary provisions, which I have outlined more in my testimony, and I think you are pretty aware of, are needed if the agreement is to provide assurances about the absence of secret nuclear activities and facilities. One of the major worries is that in the future Iran will seek to build a secret gas centrifuge plant or other nuclear facilities.

One condition that actually has evolved and that was not expected I think is the recognition that U.N. Security Council sanctions on proliferation-sensitive goods will need to continue through the duration of the deal, and they will need to be enforced rigorously while allowing verified exemptions for authorized nuclear programs.

With adequate limits on Iran's nuclear capabilities and activities, combined with intrusive verification, we can be guaranteed that whatever path to nuclear weapons Iran may pursue in the future, its efforts will be visible and time-consuming with little chance of success. However, without these limitations on Iran's nuclear programs and expanded verification conditions, a long-term deal will likely fail or exasperate the threat from Iran.

Unfortunately, I have to say that of the conditions I have stated, Iran has essentially rejected all of them and has not been willing to even come, I would say, even half way to meeting those conditions. And I must say I am not an Iran expert. I think it is almost anyone's guess whether Iran will make the necessary concessions by March 25 to seal a good deal. And the basic problem remains that the sanctions have gotten Iran to the negotiating table but have not gotten Iran to make the necessary concessions. And their internal political system and their commitments to nuclear make you wonder whether they are actually interested in the kind of deal the United States feels it needs.

Now, a risk to the United States is that the negotiations get drawn into proposing compromise after compromise while Iran just says no. Today it is more suitable for the United States to stick to its core demands that can ensure a good deal.

And I think, Mr. Chairman and Ranking Member Corker, you outlined some problems, some concessions that essentially have been made, and I would just like to highlight the one where the administration, based on public statements, has gone from wanting 1,500 IR–1 centrifuges in place in a final deal to having up to 4,000 to 5,000 centrifuges. Now, this may be justified. Such an increase in the allowable centrifuges would be accompanied by Iran committing to significant reductions in its low-enriched uranium stock, and that would be demonstrated by shipping that material out of Iran. And those two steps combined, increasing centrifuges, drastically lowering the low-enriched uranium stocks, could preserve a 1-year breakout time. But again, Iran has been unwilling to entertain either of those concessions. And I would say it is going to be hard for the United States, even if Iran is unwilling to entertain those concessions, to go back to arguing that it is only going to accept 1,500 centrifuges.

Now, I think personally the United States has developed enough creative compromises and discussed them with Iran. It is time to simply wait for Iran to make a realistic offer. The United States can then say yes or no. More importantly, it can start to more realistically evaluate if Iran is even willing to make a good deal.

While waiting, one signal the United States should send is that it is more than willing to reimpose suspended sanctions and move to impose new ones if an adequate deal is not forthcoming.

Thank you.

[The prepared statement of Mr. Albright follows:]

PREPARED STATEMENT OF DAVID ALBRIGHT

Iran and the P5+1 group of countries (the United States, Britain, France, Germany, Russia, and China) have once again extended their negotiations in pursuit of a final, comprehensive solution on Iran's nuclear program under the Joint Plan of Action (JPA). The November 2013 JPA set out a process aimed at limiting Iran's nuclear program in exchange for relief from economic and financial sanctions. On a separate but linked negotiating track, Iran and the International Atomic Energy Agency (IAEA) have been working on a step-wise approach to address the IAEA's concerns, particularly those about the alleged past and possibly on-going military dimensions (or so-called PMD) of Iran's nuclear program. However, this process has stalled and Iran has become increasingly resistant to addressing the IAEA's concerns. Whether and how Iran complies with the IAEA's concerns is currently being played out in the context of P5+1/Iran negotiations.

Despite some progress in the negotiations, much reportedly remains to be settled. The primary goal of a comprehensive solution is to ensure that Iran's nuclear program is indeed peaceful, against a background of two decades of Iran deceiving the IAEA about its nuclear programs, including military nuclear programs. This long history of deception and violations places additional burdens on achieving a verifiable long term agreement, including the need for any agreement to last for about 20 years.

A good deal should increase significantly the time needed to produce enough nuclear explosive material for a nuclear weapon, typically known as a breakout timeline. The United States reportedly often talks about achieving breakout times of 1 year. To achieve such a breakout time, Iran will need to limit specific, existing nuclear capabilities, including reducing significantly the number of its centrifuges and the size of its uranium and low enriched uranium stocks, and limiting its centrifuge R&D programs.

A sound deal will also require Iran to verifiably address the IAEA's concerns about its past and possibly ongoing work on nuclear weapons, which means Iran must address those concerns in a concrete manner before a deal is finalized or any relief from economic or financial sanctions occurs. In the latter case, a deal could be signed and followed by an implementation period during which Iran would implement its key commitments, including addressing the IAEA's concerns, before key economic and financial sanctions are relaxed.

The agreement will need to include verification provisions that go beyond the IAEA's Additional Protocol. These supplementary provisions will need to create a critical baseline of information, including how many centrifuges Iran has made, how much natural uranium it has produced and is producing annually, and its inventory of raw materials and equipment for its centrifuge program. This baseline is necessary if the agreement is to provide assurances about the absence of secret nuclear activities and facilities.

United Nations Security Council sanctions on proliferation sensitive goods will need to continue. They will need to be enforced rigorously, while allowing verified exemptions for authorized nuclear programs.

The annex to my testimony contains a more detailed discussion of key necessary provisions in a long-term agreement.

Without these limitations on Iran's nuclear programs and expanded verification conditions, a long-term deal will likely fail or exacerbate the threat from Iran. However, an adequate agreement is possible and within reach of the United States and its negotiating partners.

ADEQUATE REACTION TIME

A key goal of the negotiations is to ensure that any deal provides adequate reaction time, namely, adequate time to respond diplomatically and internationally to stop Iran if it does decide to renege on its commitments and build nuclear weapons. According to Under Secretary of State Wendy Sherman, ''We must be confident that any effort by Tehran to break out of its obligations will be so visible and time-consuming that the attempt would have no chance of success.'' [1] That goal must be at the core of any agreement.

Obtaining adequate reaction time requires that limitations are placed on Iran's sensitive nuclear programs, adequate verification is ensured, and concrete progress has been demonstrated that Iran will address the IAEA's concerns about its past and possibly ongoing nuclear weapons efforts. Because of Iran's long history of non-compliance with its safeguards obligations, a deal must last long enough, on order of 20 years, so that there is little risk of Iran seeking nuclear weapons.

COVERING ALL BREAKOUT PATHS TO THE BOMB

If Iran were to make the political decision to produce a nuclear weapon after signing a comprehensive nuclear deal, it is not possible to guess how it may proceed. Iran may use its declared nuclear facilities to secretly make enough highly enriched uranium (HEU) or plutonium for a bomb or it may build covert sites to make the HEU or separate the plutonium. Given that Iran has such a long history of building and conducting secret nuclear activities, U.S. negotiators need to take a broad view and secure a deal that makes all of Iran's paths to the bomb time consuming and risky.

Some have advocated that only the covert route to nuclear weapons is likely. Those who favor this view often rely on the U.S. 2007 National Intelligence Estimate, ''Iran: Nuclear Intentions and Capabilities.'' It concluded, ''We assess with moderate confidence that Iran probably would use covert facilities—rather than its declared nuclear sites—for the production of highly enriched uranium for a weapon.'' That assessment may have been true in 2007 when Iran had few centrifuges, and in fact, we now know, it was building a covert centrifuge plant at Qom called the Fordow facility. However, that statement no longer holds true.

At this point in time, it is not certain that Iran would rely entirely on the covert pathway option for fear of getting caught again as it did in building the formerly secret Fordow facility, and long before it has enough weapon-grade uranium or separated plutonium for nuclear weapons. The revelation about the Qom enrichment plant was highly damaging to Iran's international credibility. For example, Russia became much more critical of Iran after this revelation, and the creation of damaging sanctions became easier. Therefore, Iran is unlikely to want to repeat that mistake without greater assurance of being able to successfully hide a covert program, something it likely lacks now and will not gain anytime soon if the long-term deal is carefully crafted by the United States and its partners.

Iran is more likely today to choose a safe route to preserving and further developing a capability to produce fissile material for a nuclear weapon. In the case of gas centrifuges, it is likely to seek to maintain and increase its capabilities at declared centrifuge sites, the associated centrifuge manufacturing complex, and centrifuge R&D facilities. It would view this path as the preferred one, because it can simply and legitimately claim that all its activities are civil in nature, even if it is actually hiding the goal of eventually seeking nuclear weapons. If it opts to make nuclear weapons in the future, its declared programs could serve as the basis for whatever it does next. Then, it could pursue breakout as it deems most appropriate, whether by misusing its declared centrifuge facilities, building covert ones, or using both paths together.

Thus, the U.S. goal should be limiting sharply the number of centrifuges at declared sites and constraining centrifuge manufacturing and R&D activities, both of which could help outfit covert programs. This approach would greatly diminish Iran's ability to break out to nuclear weapons. If Iran decides to build nuclear weapons in the future, it would have to start from this relatively low level of capability, regardless of the path it would actually select in the future. The long timeline to acquire enough HEU for a weapon may turn out to deter Iran from even trying.

This strategy depends on creating a robust verification regime able to detect covert nuclear activities or a small, hidden away centrifuge plant. Iran has assuredly learned from its mistakes in hiding the Qom enrichment site. In fact, it has likely developed more sophisticated methods to hide covert nuclear activities. But robust

---

[1] ''Iran's Current Enrichment Level Not Acceptable: US,'' Agence France Presse. September 17, 2014.

verification, which requires measures beyond the Additional Protocol, can provide assurance that Iran is not hiding centrifuge plants or other nuclear capabilities in the future. These additional verification measures would ensure that Iran would have a very hard time creating or maintaining a covert program outside of its declared programs after signing a long-term agreement.

It is wiser to anticipate and block all of Iran's potential future paths to the bomb, rather than guessing and choosing the wrong one.

QUANTIFYING ADEQUATE RESPONSE TIME: THE ROLE OF BREAKOUT CALCULATIONS

One assured way to quantify the concept of adequate reaction time when discussing limitations on uranium enrichment programs is to link timely reaction time to breakout time. Breakout time is the amount of time Iran would need to create enough weapon-grade uranium for a single nuclear weapon, if it reneged or cheated on the agreement. Additional time would be needed to fabricate the nuclear weapon itself but the creation of enough fissile material (weapon-grade uranium or separated plutonium) is widely accepted as the "long pole in the tent" of making a nuclear weapon and the only part of this process susceptible to reliable discovery and subsequent pressure. Other nuclear weaponization activities, such as producing high explosive components, electronic components, or uranium metal parts, are notoriously difficult to detect and stop. By focusing on breakout time—as defined above—the agreement would grant the international community a guaranteed period of time to react and prevent Iran's success. The longer the breakout time, the more reaction options we have. A deal that enshrines a short breakout time is risky because if Iran were to make the decision to make a weapon, military intervention would be the only available response.

Thus, time for Iran's ability to produce enough weapon-grade uranium for a bomb must be sufficiently long to allow the international community to prepare and implement a response able to stop it from succeeding. Typically, the U.S. negotiators have sought limitations on Iran's nuclear programs that lead to breakout times of 12 months. (ISIS has taken the position that under certain conditions 6 months would be adequate.) To better understand the implications of breakout, we have prepared a range of breakout calculations under a wide variety of current and posited centrifuge capabilities that in essence convert the reaction time; i.e., breakout time, into an equivalent number of centrifuges and stocks of low enriched uranium.

One of the calculations considers an important case, namely the current, frozen centrifuge program under the JPA where Iran retains its existing, installed IR–1 centrifuges and no stocks of near 20 percent LEU hexafluoride. In this case, the breakout time is about 2 months, which is the same as public U.S. Government estimates. If the number of IR–1 centrifuges were reduced to about 10,000, breakout time would grow to about 3 months, according to the ISIS estimates.

To achieve a breakout time of 12 months in the case that stocks of 3.5 percent LEU are not limited to relatively small quantities, calculations point to a centrifuge program of about 2,000 IR–1 centrifuges. If stocks of LEU are limited significantly, these centrifuge quantities can increase but, as is discussed below, the total number of allowed centrifuges would not increase that much—only to about 4,000–5,000 IR–1 centrifuges. A major problem is that the centrifuges would continue producing LEU, complicating the effective maintenance of a LEU cap.

SOUND NEGOTIATING PRINCIPLES

Beyond technical limitations, the negotiations have shown that the principles driving the positions of the P5+1 differ markedly from those of Iran. Any deal should satisfy the following principles if it is to last:

• Sufficient response time in case of violations;
• A nuclear program meeting Iran's practical needs;
• Adequate irreversibility of constraints;
• Stable provisions; and
• Adequate verification.

These principles flow from the effort to ensure that Iran's nuclear program is peaceful and remains so. These principles also reflect long experience in negotiating arms control and nonproliferation agreements and a recognition of the strengths and weaknesses in those agreements to date.

Iran on the other hand has emphasized the principles of cooperation and transparency. These principles are predicated on its assertion that its word should be trusted, namely its pronouncement that it will not build nuclear weapons. These principles also reflect its long-standing view that any agreement should have constrained verification conditions and minimal impact on its nuclear programs, even allowing for their significant growth, despite the current lack of economic or practical justifications for such growth. Many of Iran's negotiating positions have been rejected because they can be undone on short order, offering little practical utility in constraining its future abilities to build nuclear weapons. Iran on numerous occasions in the past has shown a willingness to stop cooperation with the IAEA and reverse agreed upon constraints, sometimes rapidly. A robust and painstakingly built international sanctions regime on Iran cannot be lifted in return for inadequate and reversible constraints.

The negotiating process has shown the complexity of any agreement able to ensure that Iran's nuclear program will remain peaceful. But by sticking to the above sound principles, potential compromises can be better evaluated and any resulting deal will be more likely to last.

SPECIFIC PROVISIONS

In the rest of my testimony, I would like to focus on several specific provisions or goals necessary to a successful deal. In particular, I will discuss the following:

    1. Achieve Concrete Progress in Resolving Concerns about Iran's Past and Possibly Ongoing Nuclear Weapons Efforts.

    2. Maintain Domestic and International Sanctions on Proliferation Sensitive Goods.

    3. Render Excess Centrifuges Less Risky.

    4. Institutionalize a Minimal Centrifuge R&D Program.

    5. Keep Centrifuge Numbers Low and as a Supplementary Measure Achieve Lower Stocks of LEU hexafluoride and oxide.

    6. Beware the concept of "SWU" as a Limit.

    7. Ensure Arak Reactor's Changes are Irreversible.

(1) Achieve Concrete Progress in Resolving Concerns about Iran's Past and Possibly Ongoing Nuclear Weapons Efforts

Despite a great effort over the last year, the IAEA has learned little from Iran that has added to the inspectors' ability to resolve their concern about Iran's past nuclear weapons efforts and possibly ongoing work related to nuclear weapons. Recently, the IAEA has also been unable to reach agreement with Iran on how to tackle the remaining military nuclear issues. The IAEA has repeatedly emphasized that the military nuclear issues need to be addressed and solved.

For years, the inspectors have unsuccessfully asked the Islamic Republic to address the substantial body of evidence that Iran was developing nuclear weapons prior to 2004 and that it may have continued some of that, or related work, afterward, even up to the present. Before a deal is implemented, concrete progress is needed on the central issue of whether Iran has worked on nuclear weapons and is maintaining a capability to revive such efforts in the future.

Supreme Leader Ali Khamenei often declares that nuclear weapons violate Islamic strictures. His denials are not credible. The United States, its main European allies, and most importantly the IAEA itself, assess that Iran had a sizable nuclear weapons program into 2003. The U.S. intelligence community in the 2007 National Intelligence Estimate (NIE) agreed: "We assess with high confidence that until fall 2003, Iranian military entities were working under government direction to develop nuclear weapons." The Europeans and the IAEA have made clear, the United States less so, that Iran's nuclear weapons development may have continued after 2003, albeit in a less structured manner. In its November 2011 safeguards report, the IAEA provided evidence of Iran's pre- and post-2003 nuclear weaponization efforts. The IAEA found, "There are also indications that some activities relevant to the development of a nuclear explosive device continued after 2003, and that some may still be ongoing." To reinforce this point to Iran, the United States in late August sanctioned Iran's Organization of Defensive Innovation and Research (SPND), which it said is a Tehran-based entity established in early 2011 that is primarily responsible for research in the field of nuclear weapons development. Thus, there is widespread evidence and agreement that Iran has worked on developing nuclear weapons and that some of those activities may have continued to today.

Addressing the IAEA's concerns about the military dimensions of Iran's nuclear programs is fundamental to any long-term agreement. Although much of the debate about an agreement with Iran rightly focuses on Tehran's uranium enrichment and plutonium production capabilities, an agreement that side steps the military issues would risk being unverifiable. Moreover, the world would not be so concerned if Iran had never conducted weaponization activities aimed at building a nuclear weapon. After all, Japan has enrichment activities but this program is not regarded with suspicion. Trust in Iran's intentions, resting on solid verification procedures, is critical to a serious agreement.

A prerequisite for any comprehensive agreement is for the IAEA to know when Iran sought nuclear weapons, how far it got, what types it sought to develop, and how and where it did this work. Was this weapons capability just put on the shelf, waiting to be quickly restarted? The IAEA needs a good baseline of Iran's military nuclear activities, including the manufacturing of equipment for the program and any weaponization related studies, equipment, and locations. The IAEA needs this information to design a verification regime. Moreover, to develop confidence in the absence of these activities—a central mission—the IAEA will need to periodically inspect these sites and interview key individuals for years to come. Without information about past military nuclear work, it cannot know where to go and who to speak to.

The situation today, unless rectified, does not allow for the creation of an adequate verification regime. Moreover, the current situation risks the creation of dangerous precedents for any verification regime that would make it impossible for the IAEA to determine with confidence that nuclear weapons activities are not ongoing. Adding verification conditions to any deal is unlikely to help if the fundamental problem is the lack of Iranian cooperation. The IAEA already has the legal right to pursue these questions under the comprehensive safeguards agreement with Iran.

Despite the IAEA's rights under the comprehensive safeguards agreement, Iran has regularly denied the IAEA access to military sites, such as a site at the Parchin complex, a site where high-explosive experiments linked to nuclear triggers may have occurred. Iran has reconstructed much of this site at Parchin, making IAEA verification efforts all but impossible. Tehran has undertaken at this site what looks to most observers as a blatant effort to defeat IAEA verification. However, Parchin is but one of many sites the IAEA wants to inspect as part of its efforts to understand the military dimensions of Iran's nuclear programs. A full Iranian declaration may reveal even more sites of concern.

Iran continues to say no to IAEA requests to interview key individuals, such as Mohsen Fakrizadeh, the suspected military head of the nuclear weapons program in the early 2000s and perhaps today, and Sayyed Abbas Shahmoradi-Zavareh, former head of the Physics Research Center, alleged to be the central location in the 1990s of Iran's militarized nuclear research. The IAEA interviewed Shahmoradi years ago about a limited number of his suspicious procurement activities conducted through Sharif University of Technology. The IAEA was not fully satisfied with his answers, and its dissatisfaction increased once he refused to discuss his activities for the Physics Research Center. Since the initial interviews, the IAEA has obtained far more information about Shahmoradi and the Physics Research Center's procurement efforts. The need to interview both individuals, as well as others, remains.

If Iran is able to successfully evade addressing the IAEA's concerns now, when biting sanctions are in place, why would it address them later when these sanctions are lifted, regardless of anything it may pledge today? Iran's lack of clarity on alleged nuclear weaponization, and its noncooperation with the IAEA, if accepted as part of a nuclear agreement, would create a large vulnerability in any future verification regime. Iran would have clear precedents to deny inspectors access to key facilities and individuals. There would be essentially no-go zones across the country for inspectors. Tehran could declare a suspect site a military base and thus off limits. And what better place to conduct clandestine, prohibited activities, such as uranium enrichment and weaponization?

Iran would have also defeated a central tenet of IAEA inspections—the need to determine both the correctness and completeness of a state's nuclear declaration. The history of Iran's previous military nuclear efforts may never come to light, and the international community would lack confidence that these capabilities would not emerge in the future. Moreover, Iran's ratification of the Additional Protocol or acceptance of additional verification conditions, while making the IAEA's verification task easier in several important ways, would not solve the basic problem posed by Iran's lack of cooperation on key, legitimate IAEA concerns. Other countries contemplating the clandestine development of nuclear weapons will certainly watch Tehran closely.

With a 7-month extension, there is plenty of time for Iran to address all the IAEA's outstanding concerns. Moreover, an approach can be implemented whereby Iran can choose to admit to having had a nuclear weapons program, or at least accept or not publicly dispute a credible IAEA judgment that it had one, and allow IAEA access to key military sites, such as Parchin, and to critical engineers and scientists linked to those efforts. If no such concrete demonstration is forthcoming during the extension, a deal should not be signed. If it is, the deal should not offer any significant relief from financial and economic sanctions until Iran fully addresses the IAEA's concerns.

(2) Maintain Sanctions on Proliferation Sensitive Goods

A comprehensive nuclear agreement is not expected to end Iran's illicit efforts to obtain goods for its missile and other military programs. Iran appears committed to continuing its illicit operations to obtain goods for a range of sanctioned programs. On August 30, 2014, Iranian President Hassan Rouhani stated on Iranian television: "Of course we bypass sanctions. We are proud that we bypass sanctions." Given Iran's sanctions-busting history, a comprehensive nuclear agreement should not include any provisions that would interfere in efforts of the international community to effectively sanction Iranian military programs.

The deal must also create a basis to end, or at least detect with high probability, Iran's illicit procurement of goods for its nuclear programs. Evidence suggests that in the last few years Iran has been conducting its illegal operations to import goods for its nuclear program with greater secrecy and sophistication, regardless of the scale of procurements in the last year or two. A long-term nuclear agreement should ban Iranian illicit trade in items for its nuclear programs while creating additional mechanisms to verify this ban. Such a verified ban is a critical part of ensuring that Iran is not establishing the wherewithal to:

- Build secret nuclear sites,
- Make secret advances in its advanced centrifuge[2] or other nuclear programs, or
- Surge in capability if it left the agreement.

These conditions argue for continuing all the UNSC and national sanctions and well-enforced export controls on proliferation-sensitive goods. Such goods are those key goods used or needed in Iran's nuclear programs and nuclear weapon delivery systems, the latter typically interpreted as covering ballistic missiles.

Sanctions should continue on the listed goods in the UNSC resolutions, many of them dual-use in nature, and more generally on those other dual-use goods that could contribute to uranium enrichment, plutonium reprocessing, heavy water, and nuclear weapon delivery systems (see United Nations Security Council Resolution 1929, par. 13). The latter is often referred to as the "catch-all" provision and mirrors many national catch-all requirements in export control laws and regulations. In the case of Iran, this provision is especially important. Without illicitly obtaining the goods covered by catch-all, Iran would be severely constrained in building or expanding nuclear sites.

The P5+1 powers need to manage carefully the transition to a time when imports of goods to Iran are allowed for legitimate nuclear and later possibly for civilian uses. Many proliferation sensitive goods are dual-use goods, which have applications both in nuclear and nonnuclear industries and institutions. Currently, the world is on heightened alert about Iran's illicit procurements for its sanctioned nuclear, missile, and military programs. Routinely, this alert has led to the thwarting of many illicit purchases and interdictions of banned goods. But as nations enter into expanded commercial and trade relationships with Iran, a risk is that many countries will effectively stand down from this heightened state of awareness and lose much of their motivation to stop banned sales to Iran even if U.N. sanctions remain in place. Despite the sanctions and vigilant efforts today, many goods now make their way to Iran illicitly that fall below the sanctions list thresholds but are covered by the catch-all condition that bans all goods that could contribute to Iran's nuclear program. The volume of these sales is expected to increase after an agreement takes effect and many more of these goods could get through successfully. Unless carefully managed, a key risk is that the sanctions may not hold firm for the below threshold or catch-all goods. Stopping transfers of explicitly banned items may also become more difficult as business opportunities increase, and much of the world de-emphasizes Iran's nuclear program as a major issue in their foreign policies and domestic regulations. This could be particularly true for China and middle economic powers, such as Turkey, which already have substantial trade with Iran and are expected to seek expanded ties. Other countries with weak export controls may expand trade as well.

---

[2] Aside from the IR-2m and a few other centrifuge models, little is known about Iran's next generation centrifuges. Quarterly IAEA safeguards reports indicate that Iran has not successfully operated next generation centrifuges on a continuous basis or in significant numbers since their installation began at the Natanz Pilot Fuel Enrichment Plant. This suggests that Iran may be having difficulty with aspects of their design or operation. Iran's failure to deploy next-generation centrifuges in significant quantities is one indication that sanctions were effective to slow or significantly raise the costs of procurement.

Verified Procurement Channel for Authorized Nuclear Programs

The six powers must carefully plan for these eventualities now and include in any agreement an architecture to mitigate and manage proliferation-related procurement risks. A priority is creating a verifiable procurement channel to route needed goods to Iran's authorized nuclear programs. The agreement will need to allow for imports to legitimate nuclear programs, as they do now for the Bushehr nuclear power reactor.

A challenge will be creating and maintaining an architecture, with a broader nuclear procurement channel, that permits imports of goods to Iran's authorized nuclear programs and possibly later to its civilian industries, while preventing imports to military programs and banned or covert nuclear programs. The UNSC and its Iran sanctions committee and Panel of Experts, the IAEA, and supplier states will all need to play key roles in verifying the end use of exports to Iran's authorized nuclear programs and ensuring that proliferation sensitive goods are not going to banned nuclear activities or military programs.

The creation of the architecture should be accomplished during the negotiations of the long-term deal, although its implementation may need to wait. It will be important that the architecture, whether or not implemented later, be established at the very beginning of the implementation of the long-term agreement in order to adequately deal with this issue. In essence, the creation of the architecture should not be left to later.

The reason for creating a verified procurement channel is that Iran's legitimate nuclear activities may need imports. The "modernization" of the Arak reactor would probably involve the most imports, depending on the extent to which international partners are involved. A sensitive area will be any imports, whether equipment, material, or technologies, which are associated with the heavy water portion of the reactor, in the case that the reactor is not converted to light water. Another sensitive set of possible imports involves goods related to the separation of radionuclides from irradiated targets, although goods for reprocessing; i.e., separating plutonium from irradiated fuel or targets, would be banned since Iran is expected to commit in the long-term agreement not to conduct reprocessing. Nonetheless, allowed imports could include goods that would be close in capability to those used in reprocessing, since the boundary in this area between sensitive and nonsensitive equipment is very thin. These goods will therefore require careful monitoring. Iran's centrifuge program, if reduced in scale to the levels required for U.S. acceptance of a deal, will result in a large excess stockpile of key goods for IR–1 centrifuges. This stock should last for many years, eliminating the need for most imports. Nonetheless, the centrifuge program may need certain spare parts, raw materials, or replacement equipment. If Iran continues centrifuge research and development, that program may require sensitive raw materials and equipment. Needless to say, the goods exported to Iran's centrifuge programs will require careful monitoring as to their use and long-term fate.

Iran's nonnuclear civilian industries and institutions may also want to purchase dual-use goods covered by the sanctions, but this sector should not expect to be exempted from sanctions during the duration of the deal or at least until late in the deal. Iran must prove it is fully complying with the agreement and will not abuse a civilian sector exemption to obtain banned goods for its nuclear, missile, or other military programs. With renewed economic activity and as part of efforts to expand the high-tech civilian sector, Iranian companies and institutions engaged in civilian, nonnuclear activities can be expected to seek these goods, several of which would be covered by the catch-all condition of the resolutions. Examples of dual-use goods would be carbon fiber, vacuum pumps, valves, computer control equipment, raw materials, subcomponents of equipment, and other proliferation sensitive goods. Currently, these civil industries (Iran's petrochemical and automotive industries are two such examples) are essentially denied many of these goods under the UNSC resolutions and related unilateral and multilateral sanctions. However, if civilian industries are to be eventually exempted from the sanctions, this exemption must be created with special care, implemented no sooner than many years into the agreement, and monitored especially carefully. Iran could exploit this exemption to obtain goods illicitly for banned activities. It could approach suppliers claiming the goods are for civil purposes but in fact they would be for banned nuclear or military programs. Such a strategy is exactly what Iran's nuclear program has pursued illicitly for many years, including cases where goods were procured under false pretenses by the Iranian oil and gas industry for the nuclear program. There are also many examples of illicit Iranian procurements for its nuclear program where Iranian and other trading companies misrepresented the end use to suppliers.

This architecture covering proliferation sensitive goods should remain in place for the duration of the comprehensive agreement. The six powers must carefully plan for eventualities now and design and implement an architecture that prevents future Iranian illicit procurements under a comprehensive agreement.

(3) Render Excess Centrifuges Less Risky

If Iran accepts a sharp limit on the number of centrifuges that would enrich uranium in a comprehensive deal, what about the excess centrifuges? If the limit is about 4,000 IR–1 centrifuges, Iran would need to dismantle or render unusable over 14,000 IR–1 centrifuges and over 1,000 of the more advanced IR–2m centrifuges. These 1,000 IR–2m centrifuges are equivalent of about 3,000–5,000 IR–1 centrifuges. Thus, Iran would need to eliminate a large fraction of its centrifuge program.

The centrifuges in excess of a limit should ideally be destroyed. Otherwise, Iran could reinstall them, building back to its original enrichment capacity of over 20,000 swu per year. This restoration of capacity would lead to very short breakout times, far less than a year.

However, rather than focusing on negotiating the destruction of excess centrifuges, the P5+1 negotiators appear to be seeking a different solution. They have reportedly been focusing on the removal and monitored storage of key centrifuge equipment in such a way that reinstallation would be difficult and time-consuming. However, accomplishing build-back timeframes of 6 to 12 months can be difficult to achieve in practice.

Complicating this approach and highlighting its risks, Iran's reneging on a cap in centrifuges and moving to reinstall them may happen outside of any overt nuclear weapons breakout. Iran may argue that the United States has not delivered on its commitments and build back up its number of centrifuges in retaliation. By assuaging the international community that it is not breaking out, Iran may make any meaningful U.S. response difficult.

Some analysts, including those at ISIS, have discussed imposing essentially what have been called in the North Korean context ''disablement'' steps, which would not involve the destruction of any equipment but delay the restart of installed centrifuges. However, ISIS's attempts to define disablement steps on the centrifuge plants appear to be reversible in less than 6 months of diligent work. This time period applies to proposals to remove the centrifuge pipework from the centrifuge plants.

Moreover, this estimated time for reassembling the centrifuge cascades remains uncertain, and it could be shorter. There is no practical experience in disabling centrifuge plants; North Korea's centrifuge program was not subject to disablement. It needs to be pointed out that some U.S. policymakers had a tendency to exaggerate the difficulty of undoing North Korean disablement steps imposed at the Yongbyon nuclear center on plutonium production and separation facilities. In fact, North Korea was able to reverse several of these steps relatively quickly. A lesson from the North Korean case is that disablement steps are highly reversible and in fact can be reversed faster than expected.

A sounder strategy involves including disablement steps with the destruction of a limited, but carefully selected set of equipment. For example, the deal could include the destruction of certain key cascade equipment, such as valves and pressure or flow measuring equipment. Much of this equipment was imported from abroad in violation of supplier country export control laws or international sanctions.

An agreed upon fraction of centrifuges and associated cascade piping and equipment should be kept available under monitored storage away from the centrifuge plants as spares to replace broken centrifuges and equipment. This number would be derived from the current rate of breakage which Iran would need to document with the aid of the IAEA. However, this rate is relatively well known now, as a result of the IAEA's monitoring of Iranian centrifuge manufacturing under the JPA. Iran has provided the IAEA with an inventory of centrifuge rotor assemblies used to replace those centrifuges that have failed, and the IAEA has confirmed that centrifuge rotor manufacturing and assembly have been consistent with Iran's replacement program for damaged centrifuges. Armed with a reliable breakage rate, the negotiators can define the limited stockpile of centrifuges necessary to avoid any Iranian manufacturing of IR–1 centrifuges.

(4) Institutionalize a Minimal Centrifuge R&D Program

Another important limit on Iran's nuclear program aims to ensure that an advanced centrifuge R&D program does not become the basis of a surge in capability in case a deal fails or of a covert breakout. Iran's centrifuge research and development (R&D) program poses several risks to the verifiability of a comprehensive deal. Throughout the duration of a long-term comprehensive agreement, Iran's centrifuge R&D program should be limited to centrifuges with capabilities comparable to the

15

current IR–2m centrifuge. The numbers of centrifuges spinning in development cascades should be kept to at most a few cascades, and these cascades should have limited numbers of centrifuges.

An open-ended Iranian centrifuge R&D program aimed at developing more sophisticated centrifuges than the IR–2m makes little economic sense. Iran will not be able to produce enriched uranium competitive with that produced by exporting countries such as Russia or URENCO during the next several decades, if ever. Therefore, Iran's investment in a large centrifuge R&D program would be a waste of time and resources. Moreover, the goal of a long-term agreement is to eventually integrate Iran into the international civilian nuclear order (even as a nonexporting producer of enriched uranium). This integration would render mute Iran's claims for self-sufficiency in enriched uranium production or for continuing the program out of national pride.

A long-term agreement should reinforce sound economic principles universally accepted in the world's nuclear programs, all of which are deeply interconnected through an international supply chain based on reactor suppliers and enriched uranium fuel requirements. Building an agreement catering to open-ended, economically unrealistic ambitions is both unnecessary and counterproductive, and also sets dangerous precedents for other potential proliferant states.

Iran's development of more advanced centrifuges would also significantly complicate the verification of a long-term agreement. In a breakout or cheating scenario, Iran would need far fewer of these advanced centrifuges in a clandestine plant to make weapon-grade uranium than in one using IR–1 centrifuges. For example, Iran recently claimed it has done initial work on a centrifuge, called the IR–8, reportedly able to produce enriched uranium at a level 16 times greater than the IR–1 centrifuge. Such a centrifuge, if fully developed, would allow Iran to build a centrifuge plant with one-sixteenth as many centrifuges. Currently, Iran has about 18,000 IR–1 centrifuges, and in a breakout it could produce enough weapon-grade uranium for a nuclear weapon in about 2 months, according to both U.S. and ISIS estimates. So, instead of needing 18,000 IR–1 centrifuges to achieve this rapid production of weapon-grade uranium, it would need only 1,125 advanced ones to produce as much weapon-grade uranium in the same time. Thus, equipped with more advanced centrifuges Iran would need far fewer centrifuges than if it had to use IR–1 centrifuges, permitting a smaller, easier to hide centrifuge manufacturing complex and far fewer procurements of vital equipment overseas. If Iran made the decision to break out to nuclear weapons, the advanced centrifuges would greatly simplify its ability to build a covert centrifuge plant that would be much harder to detect in a timely manner allowing an international response able to stop Iran from succeeding in building nuclear weapons.

Advanced centrifuges bring with them significant verification challenges that complicate the development of an adequate verification system. Even with an intrusive system that goes beyond the Additional Protocol, IAEA inspectors would be challenged to find such small centrifuge manufacturing sites, detect the relatively few secret procurements from abroad, or find a small, clandestine centrifuge plant outfitted with these advanced centrifuges. Moreover, with such a small plant needing to be built, Iran would also have a far easier time hiding it from Western intelligence agencies.

(5) Keep Centrifuge Numbers Low and as a Supplementary Measure Achieve Lower Stocks of LEU Hexafluoride and Oxide

Although an important goal is reducing LEU stocks, their reduction without lowering centrifuge numbers significantly is not a workable proposition. In essence, the priority is lowering centrifuge numbers and strengthening that goal by also reducing the stocks of LEU, whether or not in hexafluoride or oxide forms. Limiting the amount of 3.5 percent LEU to no more than the equivalent of about 500 kilograms (hexafluoride mass) appears manageable, as long as the number of IR–1 centrifuges does not exceed roughly 4,000 to 5,000. This proposition would require that tonnes of excess LEU in both oxide and hexafluoride form would be shipped out of Iran. Because the authorized centrifuges would continue producing 3.5 percent LEU, this LEU cap would require Iran to regularly ship LEU out of the country after a deal is signed. However, at any point, Iran could halt LEU shipments and build up its stocks of LEU. Because this type of arrangement is quickly reversible, caps on LEU stocks, while worthwhile, cannot replace the priority of limiting centrifuge numbers.

As some have proposed, treating these two, reinforcing steps instead as a zero-sum game is counterproductive to achieving an adequate agreement. In this scheme, the number of centrifuges would be raised substantially, to 7,000, 8,000 or more IR–1 centrifuges or equivalent number of advanced ones, while lowering the stocks of 3.5 percent LEU toward zero. In one version of this scheme, only the amount of 3.5

percent LEU hexafluoride would be reduced toward zero via conversion into LEU oxide. Once in oxide form, it would somehow be considered no longer usable in a breakout. But this is wrong. Both chemical forms of LEU have to be considered since Iran can in a matter of months reconvert LEU oxide into hexafluoride form and then feed that material into centrifuges, significantly reducing total breakout time, particularly in cases where breakout times of 6–12 months are required. In fact, in these cases, when Iran would have to reconvert LEU oxide back to hexafluoride form, breakout timelines only grow by a matter of a few to several weeks. Moreover, Iran does not have a way to use large quantities of 3.5 percent LEU in a reactor, so irradiation cannot be counted on to render these oxide stocks unusable. This means that proposals that merely lower the quantity of LEU hexafluoride by converting it into oxide form or fresh fuel is an even more unstable, reversible idea than variants that lower total LEU stocks to zero.

Some background is helpful. This proposal is fundamentally based on Iran not possessing enough 3.5 percent LEU to further enrich and obtain enough weapon-grade uranium (WGU) for a nuclear weapon, taken here as 25 kilograms. If Iran had less than 1,000 kilograms of 3.5 percent LEU hexafluoride, it would not have enough to produce 25 kilograms of WGU. Its breakout time would increase because it would be required to also feed natural uranium into the centrifuges. It could not use the three-step process, where WGU is produced in three steps, with the greatest number of centrifuges taking 3.5 percent to 20 percent LEU, a smaller number enriching from 20 to 60 percent, and a smaller number still going from 60 to 90 percent, or WGU. Instead, Iran would need to add a fourth step at the "bottom" enriching from natural uranium to 3.5 percent LEU. This step would require a large number of centrifuges and thus fewer would be available for the other steps, lengthening breakout times.

Figure 1 shows mean breakout times for a four-step process, where the amount of LEU varies from 0–1000 kilograms of 3.5 percent enriched uranium hexafluoride and each graph represents a fixed number of IR–1 centrifuges, from 4,000 to 18,000. In this case, it is assumed that Iran would have no access to near 20 percent LEU hexafluoride, a dubious assumption (see below). In the figure, a 6-month breakout time is represented by the black horizontal line on the graph. Several cases are noteworthy. For less than 6,000 IR–1 centrifuges, all of the breakout times exceed 6 months. For 10,000 IR–1 centrifuges, the breakout time is 6 months for stocks of 1,000 kilograms of 3.5 percent LEU hexafluoride and exceeds 6 months for lesser amounts of LEU. For 14,000 centrifuges, when the stock is below about 500 kilograms of 3.5 percent enriched uranium hexafluoride, the breakout time is 6 months or more. For 18,000 centrifuges, a 6-month breakout time only occurs for an inventory of zero kilograms of 3.5 percent enriched uranium, a physical impossibility. That number of centrifuges would produce several hundred kilograms of 3.5 percent LEU hexafluoride every month. Much of this material would be in the product tanks hooked to the cascades and thus readily usable. So, cases of no LEU are not achievable.

If instead a 1-year breakout time was selected, the numbers of centrifuges and LEU stocks would be significantly less. For example, in the unrealistic case of no available near 20 percent LEU, a breakout time of 1 year would correspond to 6,000 IR–1 centrifuges and a stock of 500 kilograms of 3.5 percent LEU hexafluoride.

In fact, a major weakness in proposals to reduce LEU stocks while keeping centrifuge numbers relatively high is that the very product produced by the centrifuges, namely 3.5 percent LEU, would need to be regularly eliminated through some process. Obtaining this level of compliance would be challenging. Even if the LEU were to be shipped overseas, Iran could hold back sending it abroad, building up a large stock. Similarly, if it were converted into an oxide form, Iran could delay doing so, feigning problems in the conversion plant or delays in transporting it to the plant for conversion. Moreover, conversion to oxide as mentioned above can be rapidly reversed, allowing a three-step process and significantly faster breakout.

In the unlikely case of Iran not mustering any near 20 percent LEU hexafluoride, a plant with 10,000 IR–1 centrifuges would correspond to a 6-month breakout limit if the stock did not exceed 1,000 kilograms of 3.5 percent LEU hexafluoride. In 2 months, however, another 500 kilograms could be produced in this number of centrifuges, with the total 3.5 percent LEU stock reaching 1,500 kilograms and allowing a three-step breakout, which could occur in a matter of a few months. Thus, in practice, LEU stocks would need to be maintained at levels far below 1,000 kilograms, even in the case of 10,000 IR–1 centrifuges. And keeping the stocks below this limit would be very challenging over the duration of a deal. If Iran kept more than 10,000 IR–1 centrifuges, the situation is more untenable.

The above discussion assumes that Iran could not use near 20 percent LEU hexafluoride. Why is this, in fact, unlikely to be the case? Iran has stockpiled relatively large quantities of near 20 percent LEU oxide, quantities way beyond what is necessary to fuel the Tehran Research Reactor. By using this stock, Iran could reduce breakout times considerably after reconverting the near 20 percent LEU oxide into hexafluoride form. Iran currently has enough near 20 percent LEU, if reconverted into hexafluoride form and further enriched, to yield enough weapon-grade uranium for a nuclear weapon. The comprehensive agreement should certainly further reduce the size of the near 20 percent LEU stock; however, Iran is not expected to eliminate this stock, as long as Iran will fuel the Tehran Research Reactor (TRR). In the future, Iran could start to reconvert this material to hexafluoride form in a matter of months and dramatically speed up breakout.

Figure 2 shows the impact of only 50 kilograms of near 20 percent LEU hexafluoride on mean breakout times, where again a four-step process is used. With just 50 kilograms of near 20 percent LEU hexafluoride, a stock of 500 kilograms of 3.5 percent LEU hexafluoride, and 10,000 IR–1 centrifuges, breakout time would be 6 months. For comparison, in the case of no near 20 percent LEU discussed above, 10,000 IR–1 centrifuges could achieve a 6-month breakout only with a stock of 1,000 kilograms of 3.5 percent LEU hexafluoride. So, 50 kilograms of near 20 percent LEU hexafluoride is equivalent to roughly 500 kilograms of 3.5 percent LEU hexafluoride. If a stock of 50 kilograms of near 20 percent LEU hexafluoride is used in conjunction with a stock of 1,000 kilograms of 3.5 percent LEU hexafluoride, Iran would have enough LEU hexafluoride to use a three-step process to break out and achieve breakout times of a few months.

So, in a realistic case whereby Iran would need to accumulate only 50 kilograms of near 20 percent LEU hexafluoride, a 6-month breakout would correspond to 10,000 IR–1 centrifuges and a stock of 3.5 percent LEU that could not exceed 500 kilograms. While in theory this limit could be maintained, in practice that is highly unlikely. Each month, such a plant would produce almost 250 kilograms of 3.5 percent LEU hexafluoride. In 2 months, Iran could exceed the cap by 500 kilograms, reaching a total of 1,000 kilograms of 3.5 percent LEU hexafluoride, or enough if used in combination with the near 20 percent LEU hexafluoride stock to reduce breakout times to about 4 months, all the while claiming that some reasonable problems prevent it from removing the excess material.

If instead a 1-year breakout time was selected, the numbers of centrifuges and LEU stocks would again be significantly less. For example, a breakout time of 1 year would correspond to 6,000 IR–1 centrifuges and a stock of about 200 kilograms of 3.5 percent LEU hexafluoride. In the case of 4,000 IR–1 centrifuges, the breakout time would be about 12 months with about 700 kilograms of 3.5 percent LEU hexafluoride. If the LEU limit was set at about 500 kilograms of 3.5 percent hexafluoride, and given that a limit could easily be exceeded by a few hundred kilograms, the numbers of IR–1 centrifuges should not exceed 4,000–5000.

In sum, lowering stocks in support of the fundamental goal of sharply limiting centrifuge numbers is a useful measure that would strengthen a deal. If stockpile limits are exceeded, that violation would pose minimal risk to the agreement as long as the centrifuge numbers are small.

(6) Beware the Concept of ''SWU'' as a Limit

Enrichment effort is measured in separative work units (SWU). However, setting limits on the annual SWU of a centrifuge plant has several problems. One is that determining the annual SWU of a centrifuge plant is difficult, and its average value can change. Iran for example suggested in the negotiations that it would be willing to reduce the speed of its centrifuges and the amount of natural uranium fed into the centrifuge cascades, while it kept the same number of centrifuges. Both of these measures would reduce the annual SWU of the centrifuge plants, potentially significantly, even reduce it by a third of its existing enrichment output. But in a day, Iran could reduce these steps and reclaim its original enrichment capability; it is easy to increase the speed and the feed rate. Not surprisingly, Western negotiators soundly rejected this proposal.

While SWU has a role to play in determining the equivalence of different types of centrifuges, it should not be a limit in its own right.

(7) Ensure the Arak Reactor's Changes are Irreversible

Iran appears to accept that it must limit plutonium production in the heavy water Arak nuclear reactor (IR–40), which is almost 90 percent complete and under a construction moratorium because of the interim nuclear deal. As presently designed, the reactor can be used relatively easily to make weapon-grade plutonium, at a production rate of up to about nine kilograms a year. This plutonium could later be separated and used in nuclear weapons.

Strategies for lowering plutonium production have been discussed publicly, where the reactor would use 5-percent enriched uranium fuel instead of natural uranium fuel and its power would be reduced by more than half, from 40 megawatts-thermal (MWth) to 10–20 MWth. This strategy would involve placing LEU fuel in a small fraction of the fuel channels in a large vessel—often called a ''calandria''—through which the heavy water moderator and coolant flows. The Arak calandria has about 175 fuel and control rod channels. The LEU would be inserted into the middle section of the calandria with the majority of channels left empty. There are two problems remaining in this strategy, namely whether the calandria would be replaced with one sized for LEU fuel, and the heat exchangers would be downsized appropriately to those needed for a 10–20 MWth reactor.

Although the outcomes of reduced power and enriched uranium fuel are preferred, leaving Iran with an unmodified Arak calandria and its original heat exchangers constitutes an unacceptable proposal. If the core and heat exchangers were left intact, Iran could in a straightforward manner switch back to a natural uranium core and 40 MWth of power, undoing this limitation on plutonium production. This reconversion could occur in the open and under IAEA safeguards where Iran creates some pretext. In terms of the natural uranium fuel, Iran has already made significant progress on preparing a core load of natural uranium fuel, which could be finished, or the experience used to fabricate another one. Once switched back, Iran could run the reactor under safeguards to produce plutonium, even weapon-grade plutonium. Since the reactor would be fully operational, its destruction via military means would be dangerous and highly risky, and on balance unlikely to occur. Then, at the time of its choosing, Iran could breakout, having only to separate the plutonium from the spent fuel, which could be done utilizing a covert, low technology reprocessing plant in a matter of a few months. The designs for this type of plant are unclassified and readily available, and such a plant would be very difficult for the IAEA (or intelligence agencies) to detect either during its relatively short construction or subsequent operation.

At a minimum, Iran should remove the existing calandria and replace it with one sized appropriately for a core of the agreed upon number of LEU fuel assemblies. The existing one should be rendered unusable or removed from Iran.

Despite the merits of modifying the Arak reactor, a more effective compromise remains upgrading the Arak reactor to a modern light water research reactor (LWR) which can be designed to be far more capable of making medical isotopes than the current Arak reactor design. It can also be designed to make plutonium production in targets much more difficult to accomplish than the Arak reactor or older style research reactors.

A proposal to do so involves ensuring that the LWR is built irreversibly with a power of 10 MWth. This would require remanufacturing of the Arak reactor and changes to the heat exchangers and cooling system. Under this proposal, there is no need to produce heavy water, and the current stocks could be sold on the world market. Production of natural uranium oxide powder, fuel pellets, rods, and assemblies for the Arak IR–40 would be halted. Moreover, the associated process lines would also need to be shut down, including the production of specifically IR–40 relevant materials such as zirconium tubes. In return, the P5+1 could assist Iran in producing fuel for the LWR. Iran could produce the necessary LEU in its enrichment program.

[EDITOR'S NOTE.—The graphs and annex attachments submitted with Mr. Albright's prepared statement can be found in the ''Additional Material Submitted for the Record'' section at the end of this hearing.]

The CHAIRMAN. Thank you.
Dr. Doran.

STATEMENT OF DR. MICHAEL DORAN, SENIOR FELLOW, HUDSON INSTITUTE, WASHINGTON, DC

Dr. DORAN. Chairman Menendez, Ranking Member Corker, members of the committee, thank you for inviting me today to speak on the next steps to achieve a comprehensive deal in the negotiations with Iran.

Please permit me to focus my remarks on the perceptions of America's Middle Eastern allies: Israel, Saudi Arabia, the gulf sheikhdoms, Turkey, Egypt, and Jordan.

When one speaks to elites across the Middle East, one encounters a prevailing climate of skepticism regarding the negotiations. The tale that our allies tell about the thaw in relations between the United States and Iran is markedly different from the tale that the Obama administration itself is telling.

The administration begins its story by pointing to a change of heart in Tehran to the supposed decision by the government of Hassan Rouhani to guide Iran toward reconciliation with the international community.

Our allies, by contrast, start their story by pointing to a strategic shift in Washington. They perceive the Obama administration to have abandoned the traditional American role of containing Iran. They now see the United States instead in a kind of silent partnership with the Islamic Republic.

In my prepared statement, I investigate the history of that perception. In the interest of time here, suffice it to say that the idea of a silent partnership was taking shape in the minds of our allies even before the administration signed the Joint Plan of Action, the JPOA, on the Iranian nuclear question. And the JPOA, in turn, confirmed the sense of that silent partnership.

While many in Washington interpreted the JPOA as a sign that the Rouhani government was making a good faith effort to bring Iran into compliance with the Nonproliferation Treaty, America's Middle Eastern allies were more inclined to interpret it as a sign that the Obama administration was retreating from long-held positions without receiving reciprocal concessions from the Iranians.

Over the last year, five major trends in American policy have deepened the perception of American retreat from leadership and a silent partnership between Washington and Tehran.

First, our allies perceive increased coordination at the diplomatic level and in military operations between the United States and Iran and Syria. Just 2 days ago, the regional press noted that the Iranian Air Force was carrying out sorties in Iraq against the Islamic State. The Iranians, the press noted, could not have conducted operations in such close proximity to the Americans without significant levels of coordination between the two.

Second, this increased cooperation has not produced any change in the malign Iranian policies that historically have deeply threatened America's allies. To name just a few of those policies, Tehran continues to support Palestinian terrorist organizations, to build up Shiite militias in Iraq, to empower the worst element of Bashar al-Assad's murder machine, and to supply Hezbollah with missiles capable of striking all major population centers in Israel.

Third, our allies have noted the continued American refusal to build up the Syrian opposition in ways that might threaten the Assad regime. They read that refusal as proof that the President regards Syria as an Iranian sphere of interest.

Fourth, the rhetoric of the administration is frequently hostile to traditional friends. When Vice President Biden, at a recent talk at Harvard, stated that our allies are the problem,'' and when a senior official in the White House denigrated the Israeli Prime Minister in the crudest of terms, they were merely airing publicly viewpoints that administration officials have shared privately for at least a year.

Fifth, and not least, the conduct of the United States in the nuclear negotiations has confirmed our allies' perception that American resolve is flagging. When the Supreme Leader, Ali Khamenei, made clear his refusal to dismantle a single centrifuge, the administration retreated from established positions. As a result, our allies are now asking if it is not the Americans and not the Iranians who are in need of a face-saving agreement.

The alarm of our allies is worrying for a whole host of reasons, but two are particularly worth noting.

First, their alienation from the President's regional strategy is undermining his ability to build an effective coalition against the Islamic State. It is a hard fact of life that we cannot win the conflict without developing Sunni allies. On the ground, we need Sunni troops. We need trusted Sunni troops, troops that are trusted by the local population who are capable of holding the cities and towns from which we will drive ISIS. In the region more broadly, we need a committed coalition of Sunni states. However, as long as we are aligned with Iran and with its allies who have a well-deserved reputation for sectarian murder, we will fail to attract Sunnis to our banner.

The second reason for caring about our allies' morale relates directly to the nuclear negotiations. The demoralization of our friends emboldens Ali Khamenei. The five trends in American policy that deeply unsettle our allies have the effect of reassuring the Iranian leader. They indicate, among other things, that his intransigence is unlikely to provoke President Obama into ratcheting up economic sanctions, let alone contemplating military action.

With the threat of economic pressure diminished and the military option all but nonexistent, American regional strategy incentivizes Iran to hold out for more concessions. If the administration does not take steps immediately to reconstitute the leverage that it held over Iran just a year ago, then we can be assured that the next round of negotiations will result in the further erosion of the American position.

The first step toward regaining that leverage is for the President to sign a new sanctions bill that will demonstrate to the Iranians and to our allies in the region that our patience is not endless.

The second step is to dispel our allies' perception of the silent partnership. Such action begins but is by no means limited to building up an effective opposition to the Assad regime in Syria.

I thank you again for asking me to testify. It is a great honor to speak before this body on such an important issue.

[The prepared statement of Dr. Doran follows:]

PREPARED STATEMENT BY DR. MICHAEL DORAN

Chairman Menendez, Ranking Member Corker, members of the committee, thank you for inviting me today to speak on the next steps to achieve a comprehensive deal in the nuclear negotiations with Iran. Please permit me to focus my remarks on the perceptions of America's Middle Eastern allies—Israel, Saudi Arabia, the Gulf sheikhdoms, Turkey, Egypt, and Jordan.

It goes without saying that no two countries are exactly the same, and that within each country there are significant differences of opinion. Nevertheless, when one speaks to elites across the Middle East one encounters a prevailing climate of skepticism regarding the nuclear negotiations. It is my intention today to discuss the sources of that skepticism and to analyze its impact on America's strategic goals.

The tale that our allies tell about the thaw in relations between the United States and Iran is markedly different from the tale that the Obama administration itself is telling. The administration begins its story by pointing to a change of heart in Tehran—to the supposed decision by the government of Hassan Rouhani to guide Iran toward reconciliation with the international community.

Our allies, by contrast, see no convincing proof that Tehran is changing course. What they see, instead, is a strategic shift in Washington. Their account of the American-Iranian thaw begins with President Obama's decision, taken while he was still Senator Obama, to end wars. That goal raised an obvious question: In the absence of American troops, what new arrangements on the ground would safeguard American interests? At some point, our allies believe, the President decided in favor of a concert system, a club of powers that would band together to stabilize the region. But in sharp contrast with his predecessors, President Obama conceived of that club as including Iran.

While one can argue about whether the President truly entertains such a vision, there is no disputing the fact that many of our closest allies are utterly convinced of this fact. They perceive the United States to be in a silent partnership with Iran already, and to be working daily for closer relations with it.

This is no fleeting impression. It is a solid body of opinion, based on close observation and analysis, which began to take clear shape over 2 years ago, in 2012, against the backdrop of the conflict in Syria. When Iran and its proxy, Hezbollah, intervened directly to prop up the regime of Bashar al-Assad, a number of America's closest friends came to Washington and beseeched the President to organize a counter response. The request forced President Obama to choose between two rival visions of the American role in the Middle East. Was the United States dedicated to containing Iran, or to arriving at a modus vivendi with it? He chose the latter path.

At that time, it was not clear whether President Obama was consciously choosing in favor of Iran, or simply seeking to avoid a costly and uncertain military adventure. But his decision, regardless of his motivations, had the effect of giving Iran a free hand in Syria. From the perspective of our allies, this was a matter of great consequence, because Syria, to them, was more than just a particularly brutal civil war. It was the key battleground in a struggle for a new regional order. If only inadvertently, the President had voted in favor of an Iranian regional ascendancy.

Over the course of the following year, however, our allies came to the conclusion that President Obama's bias in favor of Iran was by no means accidental. The key event that generated this perception was the President's decision, in September 2013, to seek congressional authorization for strikes against the Assad regime. This deference to Capitol Hill was read, in the Middle East, as a transparent decision not to strike. At the time, stories began to circulate in the Middle East regarding a secret bilateral negotiating channel between Tehran and Washington. Subsequently, those stories turned out to be true. From the point of view of our allies, it makes little difference whether the channel was used to discuss Syria in any meaningful way. Its mere existence sent a signal of broad strategic intent.

As our allies were still absorbing the meaning of that signal, the administration brokered the Joint Plan of Action (JPOA) on the Iranian nuclear question. While many in Washington interpreted the JPOA as a sign that the Rouhani government was making a good faith effort to bring Iran into compliance with the Non-Proliferation Treaty, America's Middle Eastern allies were more inclined to see it as a capitulation by the United States. In their view, the Obama administration was retreating from long-held positions without receiving reciprocal concessions from the Iranians. In short, the JPOA became another sign of American retreat.

Since the signing of the JPOA, five major trends in American policy have deepened the perception of a silent partnership with Iran—a perception that is now set in stone.

First, our allies perceive increased coordination, at the diplomatic level and in military operations, between the United States and Iran and Syria. When Secretary of State Kerry testified before this committee he explicitly denied such coordination. He preferred instead to speak in terms of "de-confliction." This euphemism, however, is hardly influencing perceptions in the Middle East. Just 2 days ago, the regional press noted that the Iranian Air Force was carrying out sorties in Iraq against ISIS. The Iranians, the press noted, could not have conducted operations in such close proximity to the Americans without significant levels of coordination between the two.

Second, this increased cooperation has not produced any change in the malign Iranian policies that, historically, have deeply threatened America's allies. To name just a few of those policies, Tehran continues to support Palestinian terrorist organizations, to build up Shiite militias in Iraq, to empower the worst elements of Bashar al-Assad's murder machine, and to supply Hezbollah with missiles capable of striking all major population centers in Israel. In years past, policies of this sort provoked a counter reaction from the United States. Now, however, they barely elicit a peep from Washington.

Third, our allies have noted the continued American refusal to build up the Syrian opposition in ways that might threaten the Assad regime. They read that refusal as proof that the President regards Syria as an Iranian sphere of interest.

Fourth, the rhetoric of the administration is frequently hostile to traditional friends. When Vice President Biden, at a recent talk at Harvard, stated that "our allies are the problem," and when a senior official in the White House denigrated the Israeli Prime Minister in crude terms, they were merely airing publicly viewpoints that administration officials have been sharing privately for at least a year.

Fifth, and not least, the conduct of the United States in the nuclear negotiations has confirmed our allies' perception that American resolve is flagging. When the Obama administration first agreed to the JPOA's terms, it explained the renunciation of the demand for zero enrichment as a way of allowing Supreme Leader Ali Khamenei to save face. All he needed, so the argument went, was a symbolic level of enrichment. It soon became clear, however, that those who had developed this assessment had failed to consult the man himself. When Khamenei made clear his refusal to dismantle even a single centrifuge, the administration again retreated. As a result, our allies are now asking if it is the Americans, and not the Iranians, who are in need of a face-saving agreement.

Do the bitter assessments of our allies really matter? Indeed they do. Their alarm is worrying for a whole host of reasons, but two are particularly noteworthy. First, our allies' alienation from the President's regional strategy is undermining his ability to build an effective coalition against ISIS. It is a hard fact of life that we cannot win this conflict without developing Sunni allies. On the ground we need Sunni troops, trusted by the local population, who are capable of holding the cities and towns from which we will drive ISIS. In the region more broadly, we need a committed coalition of Sunni states. However, so long as we are aligned with Iran and its allies, who have a well-deserved reputation for sectarian murder, we will fail to attract Sunnis to our banner.

The Turkish case is instructive. In sharp contrast to Saudi Arabia and Israel, Turkey does not regard Iran as an existential threat. Nevertheless, the Turkish Government is deeply committed to toppling the Assad regime, which it correctly identifies as the single most destabilizing force in Syria. Thus, even with respect to Turkey, the Obama administration's de-facto recognition of an Iranian sphere of interest is undermining its goal of building an effective anti-ISIS coalition.

The second reason for caring about our allies' concerns relates directly to the nuclear question. It is a grave mistake to assume that the Iranian position in the nuclear negotiations is disconnected from everything else that is happening in the Middle East. The demoralization of our allies emboldens Ali Khamenei. It is just as clear to him as it is to the Saudis and the Israelis that the Obama administration has prioritized the conflict with ISIS over the containment of Iran. The five trends in American policy that deeply unsettle our allies have the effect of providing the Iranian leader with reassurance. They indicate, among other things, that his intransigence is unlikely to provoke President Obama into ratcheting up economic sanctions, let alone to contemplate military action.

With the threat of economic pressure diminished and the military option all but nonexistent, American regional strategy incentivizes Iran to hold out for more concessions. In doing so, that strategy has made it nearly impossible to imagine a satisfactory comprehensive agreement—one that includes restrictions on ballistic missiles and warheads, a full disclosure by Iran of the possible military dimensions of its program, and an effective monitoring regime. If the administration does not take steps immediately to reconstitute the leverage that it held over Iran just a year ago, then we can be assured that the next round of negotiations will result in the further erosion of the American position.

The first step toward regaining that leverage is for the President to sign a new sanctions bill that will demonstrate to the Iranians, and to our allies in the region, that our patience is not endless. The second step is to dispel our allies' perception of a silent partnership with Iran. That step begins with, but is by no means limited to, building up an effective opposition to the Assad regime in Syria.

Thank you again for inviting me to testify. It is an honor to speak before this committee on an issue of such importance.

The CHAIRMAN. Thank you very much.
Dr. Samore.

STATEMENT OF DR. GARY SAMORE, EXECUTIVE DIRECTOR FOR RESEARCH AT THE BELFER CENTER FOR SCIENCE AND INTERNATIONAL AFFAIRS, HARVARD KENNEDY SCHOOL OF GOVERNMENT, CAMBRIDGE, MA

Dr. SAMORE. Thank you, Mr. Chairman and Ranking Member Corker for giving me this opportunity to testify.

In my written statement, I go into some detail about the state of play in the negotiations, concessions that both sides have made. But the main point I want to make is that the failure to reach agreement on a comprehensive deal by the November 24 deadline is entirely Iran's fault. Many of the academics and pundits who comment about the nuclear negotiations gloss over this fact in the interests of being objective and evenhanded, but I think it is very important for us to emphasize that it is the Iranians, and not the Americans or the P5+1, that are obstructing a deal. In fact, the P5+1 led by the Americans I think have made very reasonable, creative, even generous offers that would allow Iran to preserve a limited enrichment capability as part of its nuclear energy program and allow it to defer coming to terms with the IAEA on its past and possibly current weaponization activities in exchange for graduated sanctions relief.

But the Iranians have continued to take unrealistic and extreme positions dictated by the Supreme Leader's public edicts. They refused to sacrifice any of their existing 10,000 operational centrifuges. They insist on a rapid buildup of their enrichment capacity to a much larger industrial scale within a relatively short period of time. And they are demanding full and immediate sanctions relief.

Now, it may be that this is just sharp bargaining tactics, as the chairman and ranking member have suggested. Perhaps the Iranians are just holding out to see how many concessions they can squeeze out of the P5+1. And now that the P5+1 have categorically rejected Iran's demands in these last round of negotiations, we will have to wait and see whether the Supreme Leader authorizes some more flexibility as the negotiations resume.

But I fear the more fundamental reason for the Iranian position is that Supreme Leader Khamenei just does not feel compelled to accept significant long-term limits on Iran's long-standing program to develop a nuclear weapons capability in part because his reading of geopolitical developments like the tensions between the West and Russia over Ukraine, the rise of ISIS in Iraq and Syria may give him the conclusion that Iran is in a much stronger bargaining position and is much more capable to withstand pressure from the United States and its allies to resume sanctions.

And in addition, as the chairman pointed out, Iran's economy has at least stabilized under the Joint Plan of Action. Even though it is still not doing well, at least they have been able to stop the deterioration.

Now, the chairman asked for some suggestions on what we might be able to do to change the situation because if we do not change it, I think we will be in exactly the same position we are today in March or in June. In a perfect world, the best diplomatic approach now would be for the United States to get agreement from the P5+1 to basically deliver an ultimatum to Iran, that either they take it or leave it, the current offer that is on the table. But I fear that the Russians and the Chinese will not agree to such a position. So I think we have to recognize that our diplomatic leverage is limited in part because of the very poor relations between Moscow and Washington, which could very easily get worse, by the way, if Russia takes another military move in Ukraine which seems quite possible.

Nonetheless, I do think there are some things we can do.

First, as both of you have suggested, I think it is very important that the P5+1 not make any new offers or new proposals until the Iranians come back with a position that shows that they are serious about coming to an agreement. And my understanding is that the talks broke up in Vienna with Zarif understanding that the ball is in Iran's court. So let us see what he comes back with when the negotiations resume, whether it shows any movement on these unrealistic positions that the Iranians have taken.

Second, I think it is very important that the United States and its allies begin preparing for a resumption of sanctions as early as March if no political framework agreement is reached. And in particular, that means talking to our Asian allies, Japan, Korea, India, who still buy a significant amount of oil, and start working with them to prepare for them to reduce those purchases of oil, at the same time work with our Middle East allies like the Saudis and the Emiratis to continue high production so our allies in Asia have opportunities to replace Iranian oil with oil from other sources.

And third, I hope the White House and Congress can work together to draft legislation that would identify additional sanctions and authorize the President to impose those sanctions in the event that Iran violates the Joint Plan of Action or if there is not an agreement or sufficient progress toward an agreement. I think the challenge here is crafting legislation, as Senator Corker said, that strengthens the United States bargaining leverage without giving the Iranians an excuse to renege on the Joint Plan of Action and blame it on the United States, which would jeopardize our ability to go back to a sanctions campaign.

Now, I am not at all confident these actions will be successful. I think it is quite possible that Supreme Leader Khamenei is constitutionally unable to make the kind of concessions that we are seeking for an acceptable nuclear deal. And in that case, we are likely heading for a collapse of the Joint Plan of Action because I think it will be very difficult to continue to extend these talks without real tangible progress, if not a comprehensive agreement, then a partial agreement that addresses some of the key issues. And if we are heading for a collapse, I think our primary objective is to position ourselves to be in the strongest possible position to resume sanctions, and that means, in particular, making clear everybody understands that Iran is to blame for the failure to reach an agreement and therefore international pressure is justified.

Thank you, sir.

[The prepared statement of Dr. Samore follows:]

PREPARED STATEMENT OF DR. GARY SAMORE

On November 24, Iran and the P5+1 (the U.S., Russia, France, U.K., Germany and China) agreed to extend the Joint Plan of Action (JPOA) until March 1, 2015, to seek agreement on a political framework and until June 30, 2015, to finalize a comprehensive nuclear agreement. Under the terms of the extension, Iran will be able to access $700 million a month from its oil exports, for a total of about $5 billion dollars for the entire 7-month extension. In exchange, Iran has reportedly agreed to additional restraints on its research and development of more advanced centrifuge models, to allow the IAEA additional access to centrifuge production facilities, and to convert more of its stockpile of nearly 20 percent enriched uranium oxide into fuel for the Tehran Research Reactor.

On balance, the extension makes sense. The negotiators seem to be making progress on several key issues, such as Iranian agreement to modify the Arak heavy water research reactor to produce less plutonium, convert the underground Fordow enrichment facility to some kind of research and development facility, remove some portion of its stockpile of low enriched uranium (LEU) to Russia for fuel fabrication, and allow additional monitoring and verification measures beyond the IAEA Additional Protocol. Extension is obviously preferable to the P5+1 accepting a "bad deal" along the lines that Iran is demanding.

At this point in the negotiations, extension is also preferable to allowing the JPOA to collapse. To the credit of the United States and its European allies, the JPOA is working effectively to freeze most aspects of Iran's nuclear program, while maintaining the key elements of the sanctions regime, in particular the limits on Iran's oil exports and access to revenue for oil sales. As a practical matter, Iran is unlikely to derive significant benefits from 7 additional months of negotiations under the JPOA, either in terms of sanctions relief or progress toward development of a nuclear weapons capability, as long as Iran continues to abide by the terms of the JPOA and as long as the United States and its allies continue to enforce the remaining sanctions regime.

We should be clear that the need for an extension and the failure to reach agreement on a comprehensive nuclear deal is entirely Iran's fault. Led by the United States, the P5+1 have offered Iran extremely reasonable—even generous—proposals for a comprehensive agreement. For example, the P5+1 are reportedly prepared to allow Iran to retain up to 4,500 operating IR–1 centrifuges (about half of the current number of operating IR–1 centrifuges) if Iran agrees to (1) disable the remaining centrifuges by removing cascade piping and equipment and (2) export most of its LEU stocks to Russia for fabrication into fuel elements for the Bushehr reactor. In essence, this proposal would achieve a break out time (i.e., the time required for Iran to produce a significant quantity of weapons grade uranium at its declared enrichment facilities) of about a year—compared to the current break out time of a few months—while allowing Iran to claim that it rejected any "dismantlement" of its existing centrifuges. Reportedly, the P5+1 are also willing to accept a phased easing of restrictions on Iran's enrichment program over the proposed 15-year duration of the agreement, thus enabling Iran to say that its long-term option to develop an industrial scale enrichment program has been respected.

On other issues, the P5+1 seem prepared to accept Iran's demand that the Arak 40 MW heavy water research reactor will not be converted to a light water research reactor, provided that the modifications to the reactor would reduce plutonium production capability to less than one kilogram a year and are not easily reversible. Finally, the P5+1 seem willing to allow Iran to defer coming to terms with the IAEA on its past nuclear weapons program—the so-called Possible Military Dimension (PMD) issue—in exchange for graduated sanctions relief. While U.S. and European nuclear-related sanctions would be waived or repealed at the onset of a comprehensive agreement, removal of relevant United Nations Security Council sanctions would be linked to satisfaction of the IAEA's investigation.

Iran, however, continues to take extreme and unrealistic positions. As dictated by Supreme Leader Khameini's public "redlines," Iran apparently refuses to accept any reduction of its current force of nearly 10,000 operational IR–2 centrifuges, beyond offering modifications in performance that are easily reversible. Iran also insists on expanding its enrichment program to more advanced centrifuges and industrial-scale capacity by 2021, when its current contract with Russia to provide fuel for the Bushehr nuclear power plant expires. Finally, Iran is demanding immediate and total removal of all sanctions, both national and international. In essence, Iran wants early repeal of the relevant United Nations Security Council Resolutions so it can continue to stonewall the IAEA investigations of past and possible current nuclear weaponization research and development activities.

Why has Iran rejected the P5+1 proposals? The most benign explanation is sharp bargaining tactics. Supreme Leader Khamenei may believe that the P5+1 will offer additional concessions if Iran sticks to its hard-line demands. Hopefully, now that the P5+1 has rejected Iran's terms, the Supreme Leader will be persuaded to allow his negotiators more flexibility before the March deadline for agreement on a political framework. A more sinister possibility, however, is that Supreme Leader

Khamenei simply does not feel compelled to accept significant restrictions on Iran's long-standing program to develop a nuclear weapons option. For Supreme Leader Khameini, acquisition of a nuclear weapons capability is a critical national objective—both to protect the Islamic Republic against the "Great Satan" and other enemies and to assert Iran's dominance in the region. Whatever the views of President Rouhani and Foreign Minister Zarif, Khameini is not likely to accept limits on the nuclear program except under severe pressure and threat. Under the JPOA and President Rouhani's more competent economic team, however, Iran's economic deterioration has stabilized. Moreover, recent geopolitical developments, such as the tensions between Russia and Western countries over Ukraine and the rise of Islamic State in Syria and Iraq, may give Supreme Leader Khameini more confidence that Iran's bargaining leverage has improved and that Iran can weather the collapse of the JPOA.

Whatever Iran's motivations, the negotiations will fail unless Iran is persuaded to show more realism and flexibility. As a first step, the P5+1 should not make any new offers until Iran reciprocates with a serious proposal of its own that accepts significant long-term constraints on its ability to produce fissile material and agrees that any comprehensive agreement must include graduated sanctions relief linked to the PMD issue. The P5+1 have already come up with creative solutions that would give the Iranian Government a face-saving deal it could sell at home if it wanted to. But, Tehran is unlikely to make the difficult decision to accept these proposals as long as it believes that the P5+1 have more concessions to offer or if it believes the P5+1 are willing to live with additional extensions beyond July.

Accordingly, the United States and its allies should begin preparing to resume the sanctions campaign in July if there is no comprehensive agreement or enough progress to justify another extension. This means persuading Iran's major remaining oil customers, such as Japan, Korea, and India, to plan for reducing their purchases of Iranian oil and obtaining commitments from other oil producers like Saudi and the Emirates that they will maintain high production to fill the gap. In fact, the international oil market—with reduced demand, low prices and increased supply—is favorable to increasing economic pressure against Iran, although we should recognize that renewed sanctions are unlikely to force Iran to meet our terms in the near term. Finally, the White House and Congress can work together to define and authorize additional sanctions that the President can impose if Iran violates the JPOA or fails to accept a political framework by March. Such legislation would need to be carefully crafted to strengthen U.S. bargaining leverage without giving Iran a pretext to blame the United States for destroying the JPOA.

Whether these measures will be sufficient to produce an acceptable nuclear deal is unclear, but they probably stand the best chance of persuading Supreme Leader Khameini to make difficult decisions to accept limits on Iran's nuclear program. In the event that he is unwilling or unable to make those decisions, these measures will put us in the most favorable position to increase sanctions if no comprehensive agreement or another partial agreement is achieved. Most important, we need to keep pointing out that Iran—not the United States or the P5+1—is responsible for obstructing a reasonable nuclear deal and therefore additional international pressure on Iran is justified.

The CHAIRMAN. Well, thank you all for your insights.

Let me start with you, Dr. Samore, and where you ended.

First of all, prior to your role here and at Harvard, you were the President's White House Coordinator for Arms Control and Weapons of Mass Destruction for 4 years I understand. Is that correct?

Dr. SAMORE. It is.

The CHAIRMAN. So you have been both inside the administration and outside of it, and I think that is important to note.

Is the advice that you just gave or the insights you just gave here—if you were still working at the White House, is that the insights you would give to the President?

Dr. SAMORE. Yes, sir, I certainly would. I mean, I supported the President's efforts to try to negotiate an agreement with Iran because I think, given the alternatives, that is probably the best option that is available to us. But I have always been skeptical that we could negotiate an agreement because I think Iran, or at least the Supreme Leader, is deeply committed to acquiring a nuclear weapons capability. Nonetheless, attempting to achieve a negotiation and being able to blame Iran for failure of a successful negotiation puts us in a much better position to mobilize pressure against Iran.

The CHAIRMAN. And we are agreed on that. At least, I have always supported the—I have seen the sanctions that I have authored with the help of many members of this committee and beyond as a means to an end, an end, getting, one, a negotiation, but more importantly getting a solution. So I agree with that.

But at some point, you have to decide whether or not you are heading to a fruitful conclusion. You, yourself, have repeatedly argued that both sides in this negotiation have an interest in keeping diplomacy going but that talks are unlikely to achieve a comprehensive deal, and to some degree you have reiterated that today.

So when I hear that, well, let us keep negotiating, and I say, well, why would we keep negotiating if we do not honestly believe that the critical elements—some Mr. Albright listed in his testimony—are going to be agreed to and that continuing the march toward sanctions relief in the billions of dollars, which we wonder what the billions of dollars are being used for—is it for the Iranian people or is it being used to further a program here? The answer to that is, well, the Iranians have an interest to come to a conclusion, a successful conclusion.

But I do not get the sense that they feel compelled to come to a conclusion as long as they can keep negotiating. Is that perspective wrong? If so, why? I would be interested in hearing is there a point that they will say, you know what, we are not getting to where we want to be. We are going to walk away.

Dr. SAMORE. Well, first of all, I suspect you are right that we are not going to be able to reach a comprehensive agreement because the Iranians are being inflexible and intractable on the key issues. And if that is true, then eventually the Joint Plan of Action is going to collapse. And I think it would be better for us if it is the Iranians that renege or violate the agreement because that will put us in a much stronger position to go back to a sanctions track.

And that is, in fact, the history of these nuclear negotiations. I mean, back in 2003, the Iranians reached a similar interim agreement with the Europeans that froze many of their nuclear activities, and 2 years later, the Iranians reneged on that deal. So I think that if we are anticipating that these negotiations are likely to be unsuccessful, I think we need to try to position ourselves so that Iran is responsible for breaking out of the negotiations instead of ourselves.

The CHAIRMAN. But that raises the question at some point if you realistically cannot expect that diplomacy is going to run a successful course, that you have to call the question. Does it not? I mean, of course, kicking the ball down the road may have you escape how you pursue a solution to Iranian nuclear power for nuclear weapons, but it does not ultimately solve the core issue.

Dr. SAMORE. Yes, that is correct, sir. I mean, the Iranians have been pursuing a nuclear weapon capability for 30 years.

The CHAIRMAN. At some point we call the question and say we have tried, here is what we have done. You are going to have a blame game at some point if you cannot succeed. So the question is how do you best position it so that in fact—I get concerned that we have gone from a position of strength and maximalist positions to an increasingly minimalist position. And my concern is that we are heading in a direction that the Iranians are induced to continue at a negotiation because it is moving in their direction, and they are getting relief. And, yes, it is not everything, but remember, the relief is not only the money they are getting. Under the sanctions as they existed, we would have required even more oil to be offset. That has not taken place. So there are a lot of elements here that are not being calibrated as to the benefit that Iran is receiving.

I would like to ask you all in this regard. In an editorial entitled ''More Nuclear Time in Tehran,'' the Washington Post'' quotes the President as saying in ABC This Week, the interim deal has, quote, ''definitely stopped Iran's nuclear program from advancing.'' And then it goes on to say in that editorial, we wonder what they think of that in Tehran. According to the latest International Atomic Energy Agency quarterly report, Iran has not halted centrifuge work at the Natanz facility as promised and has worked to perfect more advanced IR–5 centrifuges to enrich uranium. That does not seem to me to be halting your process. Is there a view on that?

Dr. SAMORE. Sure. I think ''halting'' is not an accurate description, but I do think the Joint Plan of Action has limited, frozen, rolled back some elements of Iran's program. Certainly if the Joint Plan of Action did not exist, they would be able to move closer toward a nuclear weapons capability, including additional research and development on more advanced machines. So I think we are getting some benefit from the Joint Plan of Action just as the Iranians are, and that is why an agreement was reached. Both sides gained something from it.

The CHAIRMAN. Right. But is the purpose of more advanced IR centrifuges not the ability to shorten the time to ultimately have the enrichment capability to make a bomb?

Mr. ALBRIGHT. Yes, I think I would agree with Gary. That statement is not accurate. And there is worry about their advances on the advanced centrifuges. I mean, when they went to enrich in the IR–5, the best I can make out of it—I am not a lawyer, but based on talking to U.S. officials, that it was inconsistent with the U.S. understanding of what the agreement did. Lawyers can argue if that is a violation. But they asked Iran to stop, and Iran did stop. And the interim deal confirms and reiterates what is viewed as a U.S. commitment to not see enrichment in the IR–5 or see significant developments happen at the pilot plant. But they cannot stop developments happening. It is really they are trying to stop major developments taking place at the pilot enrichment plant as this deal is extended one time after another. So I think they are making progress. It is slower.

But the other part of this—and this is probably why I think one has to wonder if this thing can just continue to be extended—is Iran is not under some kind of microscope. There is a lot of Iran's nuclear program that is not subject to any IAEA inspection even involving advanced centrifuges. And so you have to worry that there is something going on on the covert side where Iran is making advancements. And they tend to throw that in our face in a way with announcements. You know, they had major breakthroughs on the IR–8 centrifuge, for example, 16 times more powerful than the IR–1. All that work is done outside of any IAEA purview. It is not being done at the pilot plant. So you do have to worry over time that advancements are happening that are not in the U.S. interest.

The CHAIRMAN. That is a perspective that Olli Heinonen, a former IAEA deputy director, has stated when he said that Iran may be within months developing a nuclear weapon because the IAEA has not been able to fully inspect Iran's uranium and centrifuge stocks. He said the international community does not have a, quote, complete picture of what Iran actually has in stock. He went on to say Iran could have up to 4,000 or 5,000 centrifuges of raw materials like carbon fiber for their production outside of Natanz and Fordow. Is that not the type of concern that we would have in this regard?

Mr. ALBRIGHT. Yes. I cannot remember what Olli was saying there. But I think one aspect is Iran said it was going to install 3,000 IR–2m's at the fuel enrichment plant at Natanz. It did install 1,000 and then the JPOA froze further work there. They may have built all the components for those other 2,000. And right now—and the IAEA freely says this—it does not have the tools in hand or the cooperation from Iran to provide assurance they are undeclared nuclear activities or facilities. So you do have to worry about that.

The CHAIRMAN. When we keep hearing that we have unprecedented inspections, that may be true, but those inspections are not as pervasive as necessary to guarantee us that they do not have the wherewithal outside of what is being reviewed by the IAEA to be able to pursue.

Mr. ALBRIGHT. I think I would disagree that they are that pervasive.

The CHAIRMAN. You would disagree.

Mr. ALBRIGHT. Yes.

The CHAIRMAN. We are being told we have the most pervasive inspections regime going on.

Mr. ALBRIGHT. Well, I think the counter to that is that the United States is arguing to not only get the additional protocol but supplementary verification measures that go way beyond what is in place now. And so what I think you can say is that verification at the known declared sites is better than it was prior to the JPA. And there have been breakthroughs reported in the press, you know, at centrifuge manufacturing sites involved in making the rotors, inspections have gone from—or visits really. They are not really inspections, I would argue—have gone from once a month to twice a month, and the IAEA can do more choice of when it goes, in a sense pick a date when it goes, and have some element of surprise about the date it is going to pick. But that is a far cry from knowing really if there are centrifuges being manufactured there in secret when they are not there. They do not have cameras. They do not have short-notice inspection rights to go there that they would have under the additional protocol.

So I think the inspections are not nearly what they need to be, but they are adequate to verify the freeze imposed in the Joint

Plan of Action but they are not sufficient to provide assurance that secret activities are not ongoing.

The CHAIRMAN. Senator Corker.

Senator CORKER. Thank you. I was going to go in a different direction, but I want to follow up for just one second.

So there, obviously, I think is concern by everybody on this panel about what they are doing covertly, what they are doing at their military installations. Dr. Samore mentioned about the fact that there are possible violations, but you, Mr. Albright, mentioned that the IAEA recently reported that Iran has not only missed deadlines for resolving some of the key inspections issues—these are at the declared sites obviously—but had fed uranium into an IR–5 centrifuge. And I would just ask this question. Is that not itself a violation of the existing agreement?

Mr. ALBRIGHT. We asked that question ourselves, and we rapidly relayed the information to any U.S. official we could reach. The answer we get back was one country said it was not a violation. I will not name it. What I heard from more the U.S. side, that it was inconsistent with their understanding. And so I think my conclusion from that is that there is a great hesitancy to call this a violation particularly since Iran quickly backed down, and then in the extension agreement agreed to impose more limitations on centrifuge R&D activities at the pilot plant.

Senator CORKER. And who actually exposed this?

Mr. ALBRIGHT. Who exposed it? The IAEA exposed it in their report, their safeguards report.

You know, one could ask the question—and this, I think, also has—maybe it was dealt with. The IAEA did not report it promptly. They reported it in their quarterly safeguards report which is sent out. Essentially it is a public document that first goes out to member states.

Senator CORKER. Why would that be the case? When you have a negotiation underway that is obviously of great importance, why would it be reported in such a regular fashion versus flagged so that people would focus on it immediately?

Mr. ALBRIGHT. Yes. I think the IAEA made a mistake. I think so. And hopefully they will be more alert to this because I think one of the other developments in this is—you know, why did this happen? I do not think the negotiators on the Iranian side knew that the IR–5 had been fed with uranium from what I understand. So you have a situation where maybe the nuclear people are not so happy with the negotiations, and they are starting to push.

Senator CORKER. And that is the concern, is it not, that Iran, unlike our country—the way the decisionmaking is dispersed, people that are sitting at the table may not be at all involved in some of the covert activities that are taking place by IRGC and others. So that leads to other concerns.

But let me ask. One of you all mentioned that the reason this agreement was entered into is there was something for both sides, and so that is why this agreement was entered into. Who benefits most now from extensions that continue to carry out sanctions relief as we continue to go forward? Who do you think benefits most?

Dr. SAMORE. You know, it is a very good question. My guess is that the Iranians are more comfortable with rolling extensions because for them the situation is not great, but it is tolerable. They are getting some sanctions relief. They are able to stabilize their economy, and they are not having to make fundamental nuclear concessions, which I think are very difficult in their political system to make.

My sense is that it is more the United States and some of the other P5+1 countries that are not comfortable with the continuation of the extensions, and the administration has said they are pushing for an agreement. And I think the only way to get an agreement is to convince the Iranians that we are not willing to continue with rolling extensions without real progress or at least some demonstrable, tangible partial agreement that deals with some of the outstanding issues.

Dr. DORAN. If I could.

Senator CORKER. Yes, sir.

Dr. DORAN. I think there is no doubt that we are on the losing end of this. Even if you just look at the JPOA without reference to possible secret sites, they still have this R&D loophole that allows them to perfect the technology while this is going on. So the major leverage that we had was the sanctions, and one of the strongest elements of the sanctions was the cumulative effect over time. We gave that up. I mean, in effect, we took our money out of our retirement fund and had to pay taxes on it while they continue on.

If the JPOA was to collapse, as Dr. Samore said, we are going to find ourselves now in a position where they are in a position to jump ahead exponentially because they have improved their mastery of the technology. And if they have done work covertly, as Dr. Albright suggests, then they will be able to jump ahead to an extent that is going to alarm us greatly. It is very easy to imagine what the argument is going to be. The argument is going to be it is better for us to have these rollovers, as inadequate as they are, because the alternative is going to be to have them really rush to an undetectable breakout capability.

So the way I look at it, they are at first and goal, ready to run the play, and we are paying them not to run the play. And while we are paying them, they are shifting out their line. They are putting heavier guys in, better running backs and so on, and so we are going to want to pay more so that they never run that play because we feel it is going to be so damaging.

As a result of that, I think what we have to do is we have to steel ourselves up and recognize that if the thing does collapse, we are going to be temporarily at least in a much worse position than we were in a year ago when this thing started. But we cannot accept the argument that we cannot let the JPOA collapse because it is going to hurt us so much.

Senator CORKER. I think many of us believe the best way to steel us up is for Congress to play a role in stiffening things in the event an agreement is not reached.

Dr. Samore, you mentioned in your written testimony that for the Supreme Leader, acquisition of a nuclear weapons capability is a critical national objective. Now, if you could expand on that. I think most of us hear Secretary Kerry talking about the fatwa that we need to rely upon, that you know, this is never going to happen.

I do not think we have seen that in writing. You used to work with the administration. What would give you the sense in your written testimony to say that?

Dr. SAMORE. Well, when I look at the history of the program that began really 30 years ago with covert purchases of centrifuge technology from Pakistan and then up through the period when they tried to build two large-scale covert enrichment facilities at Natanz and Fordow and then the weaponization program that took place before 2003 when at least most of it was stopped, it seems to me that is an unmistakable indication that the Iranian Government under Supreme Leader Khamenei was seeking at least a nuclear weapons capability, if not nuclear weapons themselves.

Now, in terms of motivation, obviously I am not reading his mind, but my sense is that it is both a desire to defend the Islamic Republic against what Khamenei believes is a commitment by the United States to destroy the regime and understandably, he thinks having nuclear weapons was a good defense against the Great Satan. And furthermore, I think the Iranians believe that having a nuclear weapons capability or at least that option will help them to intimidate other countries in the region and assert Iran's dominance. So I think this is a deeply embedded desire in his world view and not one that he is likely to change as long as he is in charge.

At the same time, I do think the Iranians have been quite cautious, and I do not agree that if the Joint Plan of Action collapses, I do not believe that they are going to rush toward a nuclear weapon because they are constrained by the concern that that might provoke a military attack. Their approach toward acquiring nuclear weapons has been very patient, very cautious, very stealthy, and I would expect that to continue if the Joint Plan of Action collapses.

Senator CORKER. Well, out of respect for the other people up here, I am going to stop. I do hope at some point Dr. Doran has the opportunity to talk about this effect on Syria policy right now—these negotiations. And maybe somebody will ask that question. But thank you very much.

The CHAIRMAN. Senator Murphy.

Senator MURPHY. Thank you very much, Mr. Chairman.

I will take the bait, Senator Corker, but first, before I ask questions, just a few comments.

I guess I would draw issue with the fact that Iran's economy has stabilized and that they are the net winners under an extension of the JPOA. What we know is that they were desperately arguing at the last OPEC summit for a reduction in output because their economy is dramatically harmed by a reduction of world oil prices today. This very day they are announcing a 30-percent increase in bread prices for sale on the street, a sign that their economy has not stabilized yet.

Second, I think it is important to note that there are new provisions in this extension. They certainly do not go as far as many would like, but there are new provisions in this extension for more regular inspections, for limitations on R&D of new centrifuge technology. And if there is a JPOA or if there is not a JPOA, there is still always the potential for their to be a covert program. There is no way for us to have any degree of assurance, whether we are in negotiations or out of negotiations, that they are not doing something that they are not telling us about. There is always going to be a limit to our ability to see, hear, and know all.

And lastly, just a note on this critique that Dr. Doran raised about flagging American resolve in the region. And this is a common critique that by entering into these negotiations, we are somehow showing a lack of strength, a lack of resolve, a lack of influence. But American foreign policy is not built on just showing resolve and strength for the sake of the show. We are in the business of actually trying to get outcomes that advance American national security interests.

And if there is a suggestion that there was a resolve before 2008 that is not there today, I am not sure that in the region you can make the argument that it got us to a better place when it comes to the power and strength of Iran in the region. During a period of time when we were showing a lot of strength by invading a neighboring country, it elevated Iran's presence and power in the region. During a period of time when we were, I guess, showing resolve and strength by not talking to the Iranians and just passing down sanctions, they went from a handful of centrifuges to thousands, such that they are only a handful of months from breakout.

So I do not see entering into negotiations as a sign of American weakness. I think it is a recognition that the kind of resolve that we were supposedly showing prior to these negotiations was not getting us anywhere. In fact, it was strengthening Iran's hand pretty rapidly and remarkably in the region.

Now to the question that Senator Corker was suggesting, and I will probably ask it in a different way than he would. None of this happens in a vacuum. We are talking about JPOA and extension of it at the same time that we are engaged in an epic fight against a menacing terrorist organization in Iraq and Syria. Secretary Kerry reiterated today that we are not engaging in military coordination with the Iranians, but at the same time, we do not have a lot of interest in running at cross purposes with them inside Iraq. And ultimately we need to be on the same page with them in Syria. We clearly are not today, but if we want any type of negotiated political solution there, ultimately it will be the Iranians in part that are going to bring together the elements of that ultimate agreement or transition of power.

And so I guess my question is this, and I will just ask it down the panel. Dr. Samore, you can answer and others can. If we walked away from negotiations, if we just said this is it, at the end of this JPOA, we are shutting it down, ratcheting up sanctions, what is the impact of our policy—of our fight against the terrorist threat in Iraq and in Syria? What happens if we are all of a sudden in a newly antagonistic relationship with Iran that may involve military confrontation, maybe just involves increase of sanctions? What does that mean to our ability to ultimately get to our goal right next door, which is rooting out ISIS?

Dr. SAMORE. That is a very good question, Senator, and one well worth thinking about if I am right that we are heading for a collapse of the JPOA.

The first thing to say is that I think we are not getting very much cooperation with Iran anyway on our strategy against ISIS.

And in particular, my sense is that the Iranians are obstructing to some extent our efforts to persuade the new Iraqi Prime Minister, al-Abati, to make some political accommodation with the Sunnis because Iran prefers the government in Baghdad to be weak and dominated by the Shia, and I think they are uncomfortable with our efforts to try to create a real unity government. So presumably even if the nuclear talks succeed, Iran is likely to continue to oppose what we are trying to do politically.

The other concern I have is that up to now my impression is that the Shia militia who operate to some extent under Iran's orders have instructions not to harm any of the Americans that are present on the ground. I can imagine if the nuclear deal collapses, one way the Iranians might try to retaliate is to resume attacks on Americans in Iraq, which of course they did throughout our entire occupation. So I could easily imagine that there would be more tensions between the United States and Iran over both Iraq and Syria if the nuclear deal falls apart or the nuclear negotiations fall apart.

Dr. DORAN. I wonder if I might, Senator, address what you said——

Senator MURPHY. Sure.

Dr. DORAN [continuing]. Your initial comments about the resolve and being steadfast.

The issue is not showing resolve for the sake of resolve. The issue is negotiating intelligently. And I think that in my view the JPOA has been a ceding of leverage from the United States to the Iranians. That is the problem with it. It is not that we sat down to negotiate. It is that we had a position of strength in 2013 because of the sanctions, a tremendous position of strength, and we undermined our own position.

We also had a very strong legal position. We had the six Security Council resolutions that called for zero enrichment, and the JPOA gave that away which is a permanent concession. We are never going to go back to that. We ceded something permanent and powerful legally in return for temporary concessions and easily reversible concessions by the Iranians. They can change their stockpiles, the amount of enriched material that they have in a matter of weeks. We are never going to go back to the zero enrichment that we had from those Security Council resolutions.

I think we should have had in our mind, and we should develop in our mind now a notion of what reciprocal concessions are, a principle such as dismantle for dismantle. We will make permanent concessions when you up front make permanent concessions. When you agree to the principle that you will dismantle centrifuges, then we will give you something permanent. Right now, as I read it, it is a complete imbalance. And when you look at that, in addition to the other things that we are doing in the region like giving Iran a free hand in Syria, it amounts to a capitulation in the eyes of our allies.

Senator MURPHY. My time is up. My just last quick point is that in the vein of my earlier comments and nothing occurs within a vacuum, part of the issue was that we had allies that after the election of Rouhani would have been difficult to keep together with respect to increased sanctions. It was a moment in which we had partners that wanted to talk as well which influences that decision.

Thank you very much, Mr. Chairman.

The CHAIRMAN. Senator Risch.

Senator RISCH. Thank you, Mr. Chairman.

Let me start out by saying that my view of this whole thing is not only less optimistic than my good friend, Senator Murphy's, but it is less optimistic than all three of you guys put together.

You talked about the JPOA headed for a collapse. It has collapsed. I mean, this last thing that we went through where the new things that Senator Murphy talked about that we got—this is de minimis in the overall scheme of things.

I think what we need to focus on is where do we go post JPOA because in my judgment I think we are there. I do not know. In June, are we going to get a few more crumbs and go on again? There were a lot of us that were pessimistic about this to start with. That pessimism that I had at that time now appears to be considerably less than it should have been. I am not seeing anything here. So where do we go from here?

This is the problem I have got. When the first agreement was announced and it was a temporary agreement, then it was a partial agreement, the thing that struck me is how are we ever going to get the genie back in the bottle. And I do not see it. Do you think that President Obama is going to get on the phone to Mr. Putin and say, hey, we need to get together and do something? I would like to hear that conversation because I am telling you this thing has deteriorated with the Russians so badly that I do not think we are going to get any cooperation out of it. The Chinese are not much better. So where do we go from here? What are we going to do come June?

Even my good friend, Senator Murphy, and others say we are through here. We have done all we can do. I guess we are going to have to go in a different direction.

What do we do? Where do we go from here? I would like to get all three of your ideas in that regard.

Dr. SAMORE. Thank you, Senator.

So obviously we will go back to the status quo ante. I mean, we will resume the sanctions campaign. And I think Senator Murphy is right that given current oil conditions, we probably have a pretty good chance of increasing pressure on Iran by persuading our Asian allies to replace oil from Iran with oil from Saudi and other oil producers.

Now, the Iranians presumably will unfreeze all of the nuclear activities. And as I said earlier, I think they will cautiously try to advance their capability toward having nuclear weapons.

Senator RISCH. Or secretly.

Dr. SAMORE. Well, yes.

Senator RISCH. Cautiously or secretly.

Dr. SAMORE. Look, I think the secret threat is much more likely than having them try to break out from declared facilities because that would be detected very early. I think it would trigger a military attack. The Iranians want to avoid that. So they are much more likely to try to pursue secret activities.

And just on that point, I think we have to look—I mean, if a deal emerges, we have to look at whether or not or to what extent it strengthens our ability to detect covert activities. At the end of the day, we are going to be heavily dependent on our intelligence, which so far has been superb, along with that of our allies, in terms of detecting covert activities. But that is how to measure a nuclear deal. Does it enhance our intelligence? And I think some of the provisions I have heard of which the negotiators think the Iranians will agree to I think would give us a greater ability to detect covert facilities.

Senator RISCH. Dr. Doran, your thoughts.

Dr. DORAN. Before I answer your question, if I could just respond to that statement about the covert activities. I think one of the most important things that we need to say publicly and often is what Dr. Albright said about the Iranians coming clean on all of the possible military dimensions of their program because what we are going to find is, if there is an agreement or something close to an agreement on the table, we are going to be told that it enhances our intelligence capabilities, but it is going to be the kind of agreement that we have already heard about where we are given purview into a limited number of sites and not into other ones. Unless we have information that satisfies us about the full system that they had in place before these negotiations began, then we are never going to have the kind of inspections regime that we need in order to really say to ourselves honestly, intellectually honestly, that we are getting better intelligence as a result of the deal. So that has to be a principle up front. And I have noticed the administration moving away from it, and I think we have to hold fast on that.

With respect to your question, I share your pessimism about where all this is going. And I think we have to steel ourselves up. We have to steel ourselves up to the fact that they are going to advance in the short term much faster than we would like, and there are going to be deep problems that we are going to have in the region, as Dr. Samore said, with respect to ISIS in Iraq and in Syria. We have to realize, though, that they have deep vulnerabilities. Assad is vulnerable. Hezbollah is vulnerable. Their Iraqi allies are vulnerable if we are willing to play the game that they are playing. So we have to map out what the escalation ladder is going to look like, and we have to make sure that we are well positioned to win the escalation ladder. And we are. We are absolutely capable of winning that if we do not tell ourselves that we are inevitably going to lose if it comes to a head-to-head contest.

Senator RISCH. Mr. Albright.

Mr. ALBRIGHT. I do not have too much to add.

I mean, I think certainly I would expect sanctions to increase. I would tend to think that they would not race to expand their nuclear capability for fear of the repercussions, but I think they would build up their capabilities, and I think over time they could become quite formidable. In terms of if they decided to go for a weapon, how would they do it, I do not see it as black and white as some. I think it would depend on their calculation at the time, and if they could use declared facilities to get away with something before they are detected, they may do that. I mean, they may go a covert route.

There are some real risks there because they have been caught so many times. Or they may do both ways. So I think we have to look at this very broadly and map out their pathways and try to bolster capabilities to prevent those from developing and, more importantly, detect them.

Now, I am a little pessimistic about the post JPA environment. I mean, you can see kind of an economic coalition involving Russia, China, and Iran aiming to break the sanctions from the West. And I am not sure how we would respond to that. I think in the back of my mind I would probably think we probably better prepare for some kind of cold war in the Middle East, and it could get pretty nasty and heated at times given the armaments in various factions' hands. So I think it could be a very changed environment, very dangerous.

I mean, I think we could win that war. Maybe that is kind of jingoistic in a sense. I think that Iran is not that strong ultimately and we are, and our allies in the Middle East are very strong. But I think it is not a path that we should go down lightly.

Senator RISCH. Thank you. I appreciate all three of your remarks.

I fully concur with you, Dr. Samore, in that history teaches us. What we have seen over the last years and years is what we are going to get. It is just passive resistance. They just keep putting one foot in front of the other using whatever tool is there. And anybody who doubts that ought to read the passages in the book that President Rouhani wrote about what he did while he was sitting at the table negotiating and why he did it and how he did it and what they gained from that. I think that tells you everything you need to know about where they are going to go from here as opposed to something very aggressive to just simply put one foot in front of the other till they get to where they want to go.

My time is up. Thank you very much, Mr. Chairman.

The CHAIRMAN. Just one quick observation, then I will turn to Senator Kaine. It comes from both remarks of Senator Murphy and now Senator Risch. It is true that whether we have the JPOA or not, that we do not know about covert operations. But we do know that it took us years to identify Qom as a covert operation. And because we have a history of this country pursuing covert operations in defiance of international law and Security Council resolutions and achieved a great deal of what they wanted, the possible military dimensions element of this is incredibly important to know how far they got to understand the other dimensions of what we need to make sure they cannot go further. That is a fundamental concern.

Senator Kaine.

Senator KAINE. Thank you, Mr. Chairman.

I do know who I am more optimistic or pessimistic about as I have listened to the discussion. I am fairly pessimistic about an ultimate deal that we would find acceptable I guess.

I think some of you are too optimistic about Iran is doing really well, and in the negotiation we gave up too much, and we are on the ropes. I think we are overstating Iran's strength and understating our own. I am kind of reminded of the painful Virginia example of how General McClellan kept training his troops but he kept not wanting to fight because the South was just too strong. And Lincoln had to sack him and put in a general who knew how to fight. We have got real strengths in this situation, and they are not strengths that we have by accident.

Some of the testimony—I read it, and it almost seemed to have a little bit of an unreality about it because it was not dealing with the energy price issue. The sanctions relief that has been given Iran under this agreement in the last year pales in comparison— pales in comparison—to what they have suffered as a result of energy going from $110 a barrel to $70 a barrel. I mean, read the press in the last couple of months about the OPEC meetings and about the division obviously between Saudi Arabia and Iran and the effect on the Iranian economy of $70 a barrel oil and the predictions of many in the industry that that is going to continue for a while. They have got to have $120 a barrel to meet their budgetary obligations. They are now $50 a barrel underneath meeting their budgetary obligations, and it is predicted to go on for a while.

And it is not an accident. The $70 a barrel is caused by a number of factors, but a lot of it is American policy. We have imposed a sanctions regime on Iran via another means, and it is a fantastic one—by an energy policy that is producing more energy, that is producing more non-carbon alternative energy, that is escalating MPG and CAFE standards in the vehicles that we drive so we have to import less. By going from such an importer to now moving toward net exporter, we are doing some things that will bring them to their knees if we can continue to do it.

That is why I have been a strong supporter of Senator Barrasso— and I can say this without Senator Markey here—of the exporting of LNG and other things. I think we can use the Amer- ican energy economy to even push this even further, and anything we do in the energy space—it does not violate any term of the JPOA. It is not doing sanctions that would make anybody upset. But we are doing a number of things, and we have a number of strengths, and we ought to be proud of them, and we ought to play them. And we do not need to be too hang-dog about, oh, gosh, Iran is getting the edge on us in negotiations.

Now, I do worry about an ultimate deal. I think we all agree a bad deal is worse than no deal. I definitely agree with that. That said, I am glad we are continuing to have these discussions.

I do not know. Do any of you think that when we did not have a deal at the end of the year, at the end of November, we should have just stopped all discussions, and we should have scrapped the JPOA? Should that have been our policy? P5+1—we go to them and say let us scrap the JPOA right now.

Dr. DORAN. I think we should have, yes. Not scrapped it. I think it is very important that we show a willingness to walk away from the table.

Senator KAINE. So you would say we will put sanctions back. You go ahead and go back to 20 percent enriched. You stop all the inspections we are doing. You think that would have——

Dr. DORAN. No. I would not say it that way.

Senator KAINE. But that was what the JPOA——

Dr. DORAN. No. I would say that we should warn them that we expect them to stay within the JPOA, but that we are going to

walk away from the negotiations until we get something from them
for the reason that we are—as I said, we are showing an over-ea-
gerness coming to them all the time with deals, new suggestions
and new suggestions, and we suggest that we can be played.

Senator KAINE. Dr. Samore, should we have scrapped the JPOA
at the end of November?

Dr. SAMORE. No. I supported the extension both because I think
enough progress has been made to justify an effort to try to come
to an agreement and because I do not think that the Iranians are
going to benefit tremendously from a few more months of negotiations as long as we continue to keep the remaining sanctions in
place and as long as they continue to freeze their nuclear activities
as called for by the JPOA.

Senator KAINE. Mr. Albright, do you think we should have
scrapped the JPOA?

Mr. ALBRIGHT. No. I supported extending it. But I think the
question is how many extensions do you have, and I am wondering
if this should be the last one. Again, 4 months can be a long time,
but I think that is the key question in my mind.

Senator KAINE. Another question. Dr. Samore, you were talking
about—I think it was you who was talking about the fact that we
have had pretty robust intelligence about their program. Certainly
the reports about our work together with the Israelis in Stuxnet to
try to slow them down suggests that the intel was pretty good.
That intel continues.

Now we have intel plus some additional inspections. I credit
what the witnesses have said about the inspections have their own
limitations. We cannot oversell what these inspections are. But the
way I look at it is intel plus additional inspections gives us the better ability to target a military operation if we ever need to. Is that
not the case?

Dr. SAMORE. Yes, I agree with that. I think that we are never
going to be able to obtain through negotiations the kind of intrusive inspection regime we imposed on Iraq after the gulf war. That
is just not a realistic objective in these negotiations. But my understanding—and I am sure you know more than I do from the administration—of the kinds of additional access and information they
are trying to obtain—I think it would enhance our intelligence capabilities. But I want to emphasize that at the end of the day, it
is going to be good intelligence that is much more likely to detect
efforts by Iran to cheat.

Senator KAINE. It is my understanding—I wonder if you have
heard this as well—that the U.S. bombing of Iraq in 1998 was
more effective because of the inspections that had been imposed on
Iraq after the end of the gulf war, that the bombing that had to
be done—there was intel. But intel plus inspections gave you a better ability to target military operations than even good intel by
itself.

Dr. SAMORE. Yes, I agree with that. Of course, that was a case
where the international inspectors really did have a truly anytime/
anywhere challenge inspection regime. We are not going to get that
in these Iran negotiations.

Mr. ALBRIGHT. I think I would disagree slightly. The inspectors
in a sense are the boots on the ground, and they do provide useful

information. We know about the IR–5 because of the inspectors on the ground not because of U.S. intelligence. They did not know about it. Based on their surprise in the U.S. negotiating team, they did not know about it. So I think the effort is to have those things work together as effectively as possible. But I would say it is not to better our military strategy. I mean, it is an extremely sensitive point, and we are running into problems now with Iran because they are using the excuse that that is the purpose, and the purpose is to target and assassinate their scientists. So I think it has to be done in the context of, yes, U.S. intelligence is going to benefit, but the goal is better detectability of covert facilities, greater confidence in that the activities of Iran truly are peaceful.

Senator KAINE. Thank you.

Thank you, Mr. Chairman. Appreciate it.

The CHAIRMAN. Senator Johnson.

Senator JOHNSON. Thank you, Mr. Chairman. Thank you for holding a very enlightening hearing. It really provides some clarity. What I would like to do with my few minutes here is to try and provide even greater clarity to this issue, this discussion.

Dr. Albright, you said in your written testimony the primary goal of a comprehensive solution is to ensure that Iran's nuclear program is indeed peaceful.

Dr. Samore, was that the goal? Is that the goal of the negotiations?

Dr. SAMORE. I think the goal of the negotiations is to prevent Iran from having a credible nuclear weapons option. So that is a similar way of saying the same thing. I would be a little more blunt about it because, as I said, I think we are dealing with a country that has a deeply rooted desire to produce nuclear weapons or at least have the option to produce nuclear weapons, and we are trying to achieve negotiations that constrain those options, both overt and covert.

Senator JOHNSON. We have heard a number of times in testimony before this committee that the goal really is to make sure that Iran's nuclear program is peaceful.

It is enormously expensive to enrich uranium. Correct, Dr. Albright?

Mr. ALBRIGHT. I would not say it is enormously expensive. For a country like Iran, it is a huge investment.

Senator JOHNSON. And not only just the direct expense of enriching it, but look at all the problems they have had in terms of sanctions and international——

Mr. ALBRIGHT. That is right.

Senator JOHNSON. And to have a peaceful nuclear program, you do not need to enrich uranium.

Mr. ALBRIGHT. I agree.

Senator JOHNSON. That is what I want to provide clarity to. There is only one reason for Iran to have any kind of nuclear program whatsoever and that is to weaponize it eventually. Correct?

Mr. ALBRIGHT. Not necessarily. I mean, they have a research reactor. If the Arak reactor is modified to low-enriched uranium, they would have a need. But I think the idea is a small enrichment program, not a large one.

Senator JOHNSON. Incredibly limited. And there is plenty of research going on elsewhere in the world that says you simply do not need it certainly when you take into account the price they are paying for doing this.

Mr. ALBRIGHT. I would agree. If they rejoin the international community, they would have more enriched uranium at very low costs relative to what they spend.

Senator JOHNSON. My point being is that I am as pessimistic, if not more so than Senator Risch. I have done a lot of negotiating in my business career, and you have to first start with reality. You have to start with an achievable goal. I would say this negotiation was lost before it even started by relaxing what leverage we had from the standpoint of sanctions. Even though U.N. resolutions said Iran would have to halt enrichment, we basically said, no, you are going to be able to. We implied that that was going to be acceptable. What leverage do we have? We lost these negotiations before they even began. Is that largely correct?

Mr. ALBRIGHT. I do not agree with that. I think there is still quite a bit of leverage from the sanctions. I do not think it is a lost cause.

Also there was a general agreement—I would not say it is consensus, but that these negotiations have to be tried. If there is an opportunity where there is a belief that significant gains can be gotten, it needs to be done.

Senator JOHNSON. But we significantly decreased the pressure that the sanctions had in terms of bringing Iran to the negotiating table.

Mr. ALBRIGHT. I see it a little differently. I think there was not enough pressure to get Iran to make these concessions from the start. There was enough to get them to the table but not enough to get them to concede. With the oil prices going down, maybe the pressure will build. Maybe more sanctions, if that is necessary, will get them to concede.

Senator JOHNSON. But beginning by implying that they could continue to enrich uranium, saying that the goal was to ensure a peaceful nuclear program, that is just delusional. That is simply premising this negotiation on something that was not possible. It was an unachievable goal.

Mr. ALBRIGHT. I do not think it is delusional. I think the decision was made by the administration to accept a limited program under tremendous constraints and verification requirements in order to achieve the goal. It is also predicated on a very long duration, that you want to have, in a sense, two technical generations take place while the deal is there. You want at least one generation in a normal way of thinking. And then you think that you will end up in a much better place, and the country will not be trying to break out and build a large nuclear weapons capability at that point.

Senator JOHNSON. But, Dr. Samore, again, the only reason you have uranium enrichment capabilities is for a weapons program, by and large. Okay? And Iran wants that so it can become a regional power. It is all about power and their role in that region. Why would they ever give that up, short of just really crippling sanctions that just forces them to give it up? We are not at that stage. When we release that pressure, how can this ever possibly succeed?

Dr. SAMORE. I think the theory the administration is operating on is that Iran would accept very limited enrichment as a face-saving solution. It remains to be seen whether that theory is in fact correct. As I have said, President Rouhani would probably take that deal, but he is not in charge. Supreme Leader Khamenei is in charge, and I have yet to see any indication that he is willing to accept long-term, significant constraints on Iran's efforts to develop enrichment for the ultimate purpose of having a nuclear weapons capability.

Senator JOHNSON. Dr. Doran, do you have anything to add to this?

Dr. DORAN. Yes, just a couple things.

Dr. Samore's statement begs the question, why did we buy this theory. The theory that the administration seems to be operating under is that if we make concessions to Rouhani, that will strengthen his hand in internal contest with the Supreme Leader, who is the dictator, and Qasem Soleimani of the Quds Force. I think it is a false premise to begin with, and there is no evidence at all that that is how the regime is actually working.

I think a better premise is to assume that they have consolidated power within the regime, and they have put Zarif and Rouhani forward as front men. They have circumscribed their authority to a very narrow set of issues, and they have very definitely—Rouhani and particularly Zarif have very definitely played their hand. And whenever we have put down anything that moved outside of their remit, they have told us, no, we cannot negotiate. And we have decided to sort of negotiate with ourselves and to narrow our own frame of reference down to the Zarif frame of reference within his system, and it has been extremely debilitating.

If I could just say one more thing. I agree with Dr. Samore that we need to set ourselves up so that we are in the best position diplomatically when this thing falls apart to argue our position. One of the things that is wrong with what we have done by playing to the Zarif faction in the government is that we have muddied the waters greatly by continuing to come up with new proposals. And by doing it all secretly, we have put ourselves in a position where when the thing falls apart, Zarif is going to be able to go before the world community, and he is going to say the Americans are letting this whole thing fall apart over a disagreement about 3,000 or 5,000 or 7,000 centrifuges. Is this a reason to lose this historic opportunity?

We had a very reasonable position that we started with. We need to make that public, and we need to put the coalition together that agrees with it, and we need to stick to it.

Senator JOHNSON. We need to describe and face reality, and we are not doing that now.

Thank you.

The CHAIRMAN. Senator Barrasso.

Senator BARRASSO. Thank you, Mr. Chairman.

The American people have a right to be angry, angry that the administration has declined to provide a Government witness for today's hearing. It is time for the administration to explain to Congress and to the American people the reasoning behind the newest extension of the so-called Joint Plan of Action.

Once again, the Iranians wanted even more time to talk, and the President unwisely agreed to it. So I am concerned about Iran's ability to continue its deliberate pattern of delay and distraction. With the most recent extension of the interim agreement is gaining more time, gaining access to billions in additional funds held abroad, and gaining relief from specific sanctions. Instead of being limited and temporary, as President Obama promised, the sanction relief appears to be boundless and never-ending.

It is crystal clear that the sanctions caused overwhelming economic pressure and it is that pressure that brought the Iranian regime to the negotiating table over its nuclear program. The administration has already admitted to the fact. Instead of a policy designed to tighten the economic pressure, this administration seems to be rewarding the Iranians' continued stall tactics.

Sanctions relief has certainly failed to get a favorable final agreement. The past 6 years of failed negotiations have shown that we cannot simply talk the Iranian regime out of its illicit nuclear program. Instead of endless discussion, we need security. It is clearly going to take tougher sanctions to get us where we need to be, and that is total dismantling of Iran's illicit nuclear program.

So while the President seems desperate to announce any sort of deal with the Iranians, the American people cannot afford a bad deal or more years of delay. Without increased pressure from America, Iran will continue to enjoy relief from sanctions without dismantling their nuclear program.

So I would call on the President to make good on his remarks from the State of the Union, the 2014 State of the Union. He promised that he would, quote, ''be the first to call for more sanctions if Iran failed to complete an agreement.'' He can do two important things right now to keep his word: one, reinstate full sanctions. The sanctions relief the administration continues to give to Iran removes the urgency for them to complete a final deal. It is time to reimpose those sanctions now to renew urgency on Iran. And second, he can call on Congress to pass a bill to impose new sanctions to compel Iran to complete a final agreement before the end of this year.

So I am ready to increase sanctions and stop Iran from building a nuclear weapon.

My question to the three of you is, could you please outline—and nobody has asked this question—where you believe Iran's program stands today and the dangers of continuing with these rolling extensions? Perhaps, Dr. Samore, we could start with you.

Dr. SAMORE. Thank you, Senator. Let me just respond briefly.

If the Joint Plan of Action collapses, then I think we will have an opportunity to increase sanctions on Iran. But I do not think we should kid ourselves that we are in a position to force Iran to capitulate anytime soon. We are talking about a long, drawn-out process which is likely to take years. And I think Iran during that time will continue to gradually, cautiously build up their nuclear capability.

But to answer your specific question, I do not think Iran right now has a credible pathway to produce nuclear weapons. It is true that on paper they are a couple of months away of breakout at their declared facilities, but it is far too dangerous for them to try to produce nuclear weapons at this declared facilities because it would be detected quickly. And I do think the United States or Israel would destroy those facilities before that could be achieved.

I do not think Iran has large-scale covert facilities now because I believe our intelligence has exposed the last one they tried to build, Fordow. But I think they will try in the future.

So I think we still have time. We are in a desperate situation in terms of Iran being on the cusp of being able to produce nuclear weapons. I think, frankly, our whole strategy over the last 30 years has been to delay the program through diplomacy, sabotage, export controls, sanctions, military threats, and we have been able to buy time. And I think that continues to be our fundamental strategy in the hopes that the next Iranian Government will place less value on acquiring nuclear weapons.

Senator BARRASSO. Dr. Doran.

Dr. DORAN. On the technical side of things, I cannot add anything more to what Dr. Samore and Mr. Albright have said.

Senator BARRASSO. Mr. Albright.

Mr. ALBRIGHT. I agree with Gary. I mean, I think we are not in a bad place.

I would also like to add, though, in the fall of 2013 when the JPA went into effect, when we did our analysis, we were looking at Iran reaching a pretty bad place in about a year where they could have had 20,000–30,000 centrifuges, 3,000 advanced ones deployed, and there was a great deal of worry they were building a third centrifuge plant, which under the current rules, they do not have to declare to the inspectors until it is done. So I think we were heading to a bad place.

And I think if this deal or the JPA collapses, I think there have to be efforts made not only to increase sanctions but to try to prevent Iran from going that route again of just full-scale deployment of whatever it can get.

And I agree with Gary. I think they will try the covert route again, and we may not detect it. I do worry that our intelligence capabilities are not as great as they have been in Iran, and I think part of the reason is because Iran is learning. We do a lot of work at my institute. I hesitate to call it ISIS here, but we do a lot of work at my institute looking at illicit procurement. And Iran is getting better at hiding——

The CHAIRMAN. For the record, could you define the acronym of what that means in your case?

Mr. ALBRIGHT. Okay. Institute for Science and International Security. We had the name long before they did. [Laughter.]

Senator RISCH. Did you copyright that?

Mr. ALBRIGHT. Well, unfortunately, it is an Egyptian goddess. So it was not possible. There are a lot of Isises actually, including girls named Isis. So it is a complicated issue.

Just to go back to this, on the illicit procurements, they are taking steps to hide that it is for a nuclear program because a lot of these things are dual-use goods, and they are being sought covertly. And so you see that Iran is learning to hide things better, and I think they are going to learn to hide things better if they do covert activities.

And that is also why I personally believe that the verification side of this deal is critically important because those rules can allow you to break through the gaming that Iran does. And that, combined with intelligence organizations, can lead to a much, much stronger deal.

Senator BARRASSO. Thank you.

Thank you, Mr. Chairman. My time has expired.

The CHAIRMAN. Senator Paul.

Senator PAUL. Thank you and thank you to the panel.

There has been some discussion of optimism versus pessimism. And I guess my question would start out to Dr. Samore. Do you think it is a significant step forward that Iran has reduced all of its 20-percent enriched uranium to a less-enriched state?

Dr. SAMORE. I frankly do not think it is very significant. It was certainly an issue that Prime Minister Netanyahu raised because it does shorten the time that Iran would need in order to produce a significant quantity of weapons-grade material.

Senator PAUL. Would it be more significant if it were not an oxide but all the way into fuel rods where it was less reversible?

Dr. SAMORE. Yes, sir, because it makes it harder to reverse. And my understanding is that under this extension, they have agreed to convert an additional portion, I think 35 kilograms of the 75 or so they have in the form of oxide to fuel rods.

Senator PAUL. I mean, you can look at the glass half full or half empty, but I think that is better than before the negotiations.

Dr. SAMORE. Well, I agree with my colleague, David Albright, that if it were not for the agreed—if it were not for the Joint Plan of Action, the Iranian program would be more advanced.

Senator PAUL. As a followup to that, Dr. Samore, do you believe that Iran is largely in compliance with the interim agreement or mostly in noncompliance?

Dr. SAMORE. Oh, they are mostly in compliance.

Senator PAUL. Once again, it is optimism versus pessimism. Everybody is alarmed at all of the noncompliance. Nobody is mentioning any compliance. And I am not here to apologize for their behavior, but there are some things and some signs that I think should be looked at in an optimistic way.

Dr. Samore, do you think new sanctions legislation will be supported by our allies if we were to pass—this body passed new operations at this point?

Dr. SAMORE. I think it depends on the exact language. New sanctions legislation that imposed a hard deadline and took any discretion out of the hands of the administration to impose those sanctions would not be supported by our allies.

Senator PAUL. Currently we have a proposal that would say that they have to dismantle all their nuclear infrastructure. Do you think that would be supported by our allies?

Dr. SAMORE. No, because I do not think they believe it is achievable.

Senator PAUL. Do you think that if we have sanctions and we go forward with bare-knuckle sanctions, hard-core sanctions and we ratchet it up—do you think they will be effective if they are unilateral and just from the United States?

Dr. SAMORE. They will be much less effective. I mean, we do have the ability to take unilateral actions that other countries—if they are faced with a choice between business with the United States or business with Iran, they are obviously going to choose the United States in most cases. But I agree with the general thrust of your question that our sanctions are, obviously, going to be more effective if we have agreement from our allies and partners to support it. And that is why I have emphasized that we need to manipulate, as much as we can, the situation so that Iran is blamed for the failure of negotiations and not the United States.

Senator PAUL. This would just be a followup to that for Dr. Samore. It is that many have said and some on the panel have said, oh, gosh, we should walk away from the negotiations. Any discussion is worse than no discussion. I think it is interesting just to think about—and I am not supporting this, but to think of what if in 5 years from now we still had an interim agreement that says they are not going to enrich from 5 to 20. They still have more centrifuges than we would like, and we are still watching them to see whether or not they are utilizing and doing more with their centrifuges than we would wish to do with them. But to my mind, that would be better than no negotiations. It would be better than war with Iran. Once we have war with Iran, there will be no more inspections. Once the first bomb drops, you will never have another inspection inside of Iran.

So I do not know. I guess I see more optimism in continuing to negotiate than I see pessimism even with the imperfections of being at an interim agreement because currently while we are not getting rid of all enriched uranium, they have agreed in the interim agreement not to enrich—what—from 5 to 20.

Dr. SAMORE. So I agree with you that we derive benefit from the Joint Plan of Action in terms of limits on Iran's nuclear program, but I am skeptical that it is going to be possible, given politics both in the United States and in Iran, to extend this Joint Plan of Action indefinitely without some concrete progress. And I guess the main point I am making is if that is true that we are not actually able to continue to roll over this agreement, it is much better for us if it is Iran that loses patience first and reneges or violates the deal than for us to be the one.

Senator PAUL. I think you would see a pretty unified Congress if they are in noncompliance with the interim agreement. If they begin reenriching to 20 percent again in defiance of this or add centrifuges in defiance of the agreement as well, I think there would be more unity of action. There would also be more international, I think, unity of action if it were Iranian noncompliance. So I do think that that is a factor that we ought to consider in moving forward.

Thank you for your time.

The CHAIRMAN. Let me just take a final round here.

So, Dr. Samore, you said in your testimony that in fact—we agree the Ayatollah is the ultimate decider here. Is that a fair statement?

Dr. SAMORE. Yes, sir. I think he has the final word.

The CHAIRMAN. He has the final word. So everything we talk about to Rouhani and Zarif are aspirational, but at the end of the day, the Ayatollah holds the final word.

You also, I think in your testimony, either in the written or verbal testimony, said that for the Ayatollah, this is about regime preservation. Is it not?

Dr. SAMORE. Yes, I believe so.

The CHAIRMAN. The question of achieving a nuclear weapon is in his mind the preservation of the regime and the revolution and the Islamic republic as it exists today. Is that a fair statement?

Dr. SAMORE. That is how I read his world view. Yes, sir.

The CHAIRMAN. And is that the way you read the world view when you were sitting at the White House for 4 years?

Dr. SAMORE. Yes, sir.

The CHAIRMAN. So if it is in the Ayatollah's final decision and if regime preservation is achieved by acquiring a nuclear weapon, what changes that for the Ayatollah?

Dr. SAMORE. Well, I do not think he is going to fundamentally give up the ambition to acquire nuclear weapons. The question is whether we can influence his calculation of what risk to take and what cost to bear. And we know from history that he has been willing in the past to accept limited and temporary restrictions on the program when he thought the risk was great enough. I mean, that is the story of the agreement that he reached with the Europeans from 2003 to 2005. That is the story of why they have agreed to the Joint Plan of Action in hopes that would lessen the economic pressure.

The CHAIRMAN. But again, that calculation only changed his mind for, one, a temporary period of time and, two, only because there are outside influences to try to change that calculation. Is that a fair statement?

Dr. SAMORE. Yes. In my view the best that diplomacy can achieve is temporary constraints. He is not going to make a fundamental decision to give up the ultimate objective, but we are in the business of trying to buy time. We are in the business of trying to delay the program.

The CHAIRMAN. So let us talk about buying time because I heard you say it, and I heard Senator Paul say if 5 years from now we are in the Joint Plan of Action, that is better than the alternative.

However, buying time also means the Iranians make progress on their program. Does it not? Unless you change the nature of the joint agreement, you have a continuous ability because the R&D exception here is pretty large. So you allow them to continue to move forward.

Dr. SAMORE. Yes. I think the big weakness in the Joint Plan of Action is that it did not have clear provisions about what the restrictions were on centrifuge research and development. My understanding—and I am sure you can get a more detailed briefing on this than I can—is that this most recent extension——

The CHAIRMAN. Do not be so sure about that. [Laughter.]

Dr. SAMORE. This most recent extension does include clarity about a number of the restrictions on research and development, and I think that begins to close the loophole. But I agree with you that if the Joint Plan of Action is going to be extended for a much longer period of time, it is going to have to include more clarity on these kinds of issues. Otherwise, we will not be confident that the Iranians are not taking advantage of that time period to improve their capabilities.

But also, keep in mind, Senator, if the Joint Plan of Action collapses, there is no constraint on their program except their fear that they will do something that will provoke a military attack.

The CHAIRMAN. Granted. And that was true before the Joint Plan of Action as well.

But the point is buying time from my perspective—and inform me where I am wrong—is not endless because buying time does not truly freeze everything because unless you do a total freeze on the R&D, you have allowed them to move forward significantly in a moment in which if it falls apart or they choose to move forward, their window has closed.

Dr. SAMORE. I agree. Buying time does not solve the problem. Even an agreement does not solve the problem because I do not have that much confidence that Iran would honor an agreement during whatever the lifetime is. I think we would have to be very wary that they would cheat, as they have in the past on all their nuclear agreements. So we should not kid ourselves that there is a permanent solution to this problem as long as the current Government in Iran is in power, whatever we do is going to be a temporary measure.

The CHAIRMAN. And the final point I just want to raise here. You know, our intelligence did ultimately discover their underground facilities, but it was built already. It was built already, largely built already.

Dr. SAMORE. Well, actually I think—we can discuss that in a different setting, but I think both Natanz and Fordow were discovered very early in the construction process.

The CHAIRMAN. Okay. Well, maybe we did not reveal it until——

Dr. SAMORE. That is correct, sir. We did not reveal it until——

The CHAIRMAN. I have a difficulty understanding how it is that—how a critical part of what we are trying to achieve here was put on the back burner and seems in these negotiations to be increasingly be placed on the back burner, which is the possible military dimensions of the Iranian program, because from my perspective that should have been one of the first things that should have been included in the negotiation because if you understand how far they got, then that is part of the equation of determining what else you have to consider as to what a program is. And we do not know how far they got. And it is one of the things that they find most intractable to pursue. And that is not just our view. That is the Security Council resolution view. And yet, they have not been willing to comply with that. And the most recent report of the IAEA reiterates that they have made no progress on that.

Now, in addition to, of course, the concern about the Quds Force and the Revolutionary Guard and all of those being resistant to exposing their military dimensions, it is also problematic for the regime—is it not—to actually come forth and come clean about their military dimensions because it undermines the basic framework that the Iranians have taken to the world that, in fact, this was for peaceful purposes.

Dr. SAMORE. My view is that the Government in Iran cannot possibly admit the truth, which is that they were pursuing a nuclear weapons program before 2003. So I think that the administration is seeking to basically defer that issue and keep it linked to the continuation of U.N. Security Council sanctions in the hopes that once an agreement is in place, the Iranians will be willing to be more candid with the IAEA about what activity they carried out but never admitting that it was for the purpose of producing nuclear weapons.

The CHAIRMAN. Yes. And deferring it to the end allowed at any given point in time, if this breaks through, never to have come forth as to the possible military dimensions or as to how far they got along in that process.

Dr. SAMORE. I think very often when impossible issues are deferred, both sides—I mean, we are hoping that by deferring the issue, it makes it easier to solve. No doubt the Iranians are hoping that by deferring the issue, they will not have to solve it. But that is often the case in negotiations. The issues that cannot be solved are put off.

The CHAIRMAN. Some of these elements remind me of some of the concerns I had with North Korea and where we are today.

In any event, I know Senator Markey has now come for the first time. I will recognize Senator Corker and then go to Senator Markey.

Senator CORKER. Thank you. I think this has been an outstanding hearing. We thank all the witnesses for their testimony.

At the end of the day, if we end up with an agreement—do you all agree, by the way, that where we are headed right now likely is for an agreement that is less than 10 years?

Mr. ALBRIGHT. No, I do not.

Senator CORKER. Do you think there is a possibility——

Mr. ALBRIGHT. For longer, yes.

Senator CORKER. And based on the insights that you have, where do you think we are headed lengthwise?

Mr. ALBRIGHT. I think it could be significantly longer than—well, the U.S. position could be significantly longer——

Senator CORKER. I understand that. But where do you think ultimately we are going to end up?

Mr. ALBRIGHT. I think 15 years. That would be not desirable. I would have to take a second look if that is acceptable given other conditions in the deal.

Dr. SAMORE. Senator, my understanding is that we are proposing a 15-year agreement, but after 10 years some of the restrictions on their enrichment program would begin to be lifted. But I do not know precisely what the details are. I think 15 years is a very reasonable period for us to insist on, and I hope the administration sticks to that.

But as I said, whether it is 10 years or 15 years, we should not assume that Iran is going to honor any agreement no matter how long it is.

Senator CORKER. And we are lifting the restrictions on enrichment, which has been sort of the central concern that people have that we went beyond the U.N. resolutions. We are lifting those and per discussions today after 10 years for what reason?

Dr. SAMORE. I am not sure I understand.

Senator CORKER. We are lifting restrictions on enrichment after 10 years for what reason? I mean, why would we begin to go backward after 10 years?

Dr. SAMORE. Well, of course, the United States for a long time now, going back to the Bush administration, has said that once Iran satisfies concerns about its nuclear program, they will be treated like any other party under the NPT. And under the NPT, there is no restriction on them developing enrichment for peaceful purposes. So the idea is to, as I said in my written testimony, give the Iranians a way to claim that after some period of time, they would be free to develop an enrichment program for their nuclear power program, provided that it is under IAEA safeguards. As I said, I do not see any indication the Iranians are prepared to agree to that, but that was the idea of putting that notion forward.

Senator CORKER. And they are obviously pushing for something that is far shorter than that.

Dr. SAMORE. Yes. What they have said—and the Supreme Leader has said this publicly—they want to have a very large-scale program, 20 times more than what they currently have, by 2021 when their current contract with the Russians expires to provide fuel for the Bushehr reactor. And the Iranians are arguing, at least up to now—they are saying they have to begin building that bigger capacity now, otherwise it will not be ready in 2021. Frankly that is a ridiculous position, and as long as they continue to take that, it gives us a very good basis for arguing that Iran is taking positions that make an agreement impossible.

Mr. ALBRIGHT. Yes. I think it also is true that the United States has kind of been leaning forward on concessions and not getting much of an Iranian response, and I think that is one of the reasons why I have concluded that it is really necessary for the United States to step back because you do not want to be trapped by those exploratory concessions.

And I would argue that 20 years is what you want. It may take the IAEA 20 years, given their experience in Iran, to do what is called reach a broad conclusion under the additional protocol that the program is indeed peaceful. It is a very laborious process, and I would hate to see Iran dramatically increasing its enrichment capability until the IAEA is finished with its work. And I would not expect that work to be done quickly at all, given the level of noncompliance in Iran and the complexity of the situation.

Senator CORKER. And I think most of us began with the anticipation that we are only talking about a 20-year issue. I think as we have talked with folks, as you have all along, that period keeps coming back more toward a 10-year period, and we know the last offer by Iran was 5.

By the way, you are beginning to look at a temporary arrangement there. We talked about a temporary arrangement under the JPOA, but that becomes almost a temporary nature if you were to achieve the full outcome.

Let me just ask you this question. What from your perspective—we keep hearing from the administration that involvement by Congress will totally jeopardize the negotiations. Do you get any indication from the people that you talk with, the other countries that we are dealing with, that Congress weighing in in some fashion on additional sanctions after or just congressional oversight, Congress wanting to approve this deal before any funds can be expended to implement it—do you get any indication that that is something that would stop negotiations or cause people to walk away from the table?

Dr. SAMORE. Well, I have to be honest. I do think our allies are nervous about Congress acting independently of the administration and either bringing the talks to an end by giving Iran a pretext for walking away or blocking an agreement that is negotiated which our allies think is a reasonable compromise. So I do think there is some trepidation.

I am trying to figure out or I would like to try to encourage a way for Congress and the White House to work together to strengthen the U.S. bargaining position. And I do think we are pursuing a common objective here, which is stop Iran from having nuclear weapons, and we all recognize that sanctions and the threat of sanctions is our most powerful instrument. Now, I do not know whether it is going to be possible to craft language that satisfies both Congress and the White House, but I think it is worth an effort to see if we cannot do that, especially because we are entering a critical moment here where either there is a breakthrough or this whole thing falls apart.

Dr. DORAN. If I could. I do not entirely agree with what Dr. Samore said about our allies. I know from my own discussions with some of our partners that there is not complete happiness with the U.S. position. We do have partners who have been working closely with us who feel that we have conceded too much in these negotiations.

Dr. SAMORE. Sorry. I should have clarified. When I said ''allies,'' I meant our European allies. I totally agree with Dr. Doran that our Middle East allies are very, very uncomfortable.

Dr. DORAN. We have at least one European ally that also is unhappy with our position.

Senator CORKER. Thank you.

The CHAIRMAN. Senator Markey.

Senator MARKEY. Thank you, Mr. Chairman.

As is the case with many international issues, at the heart of this issue is energy. It happens over and over again. And to a lot of people, it is difficult to comprehend how much natural gas Iran has. So I thought I would just begin by giving you all a few numbers to think about.

The first number is two. That is Iran's global rank in terms of proven natural gas reserves. Only Russia has more natural gas than Iran.

Next number, 400 billion cubic feet. That is how much natural gas Iran flares every year. That is enough to supply my entire home State of Massachusetts, 7 million people, with natural gas for a year. It would be worth more than $7 billion if they captured it and shipped it as liquefied natural gas. Instead, they simply produce and sell their oil and burn off as much natural gas that is coproduced with it.

Final number, eight. Eight is the number of nuclear power plant equivalents in natural gas that gets flared in Iran on a yearly basis.

So this is not a question of their capacity to generate electricity for their people at a very inexpensive rate. This is natural gas they waste. If they are genuinely interested in safe, reliable, dependable, and efficient generation of electricity, they have a pretty obvious path to that. And they are the last country in the world that needs nuclear power to generate electricity. That is just the bottom line.

So my first question to you is, do you all agree with that, that they do not need nuclear power in order to generate electricity for the rest of this century, that the proven reserves they have for the population that they have is more than enough to give them all their generating capacity?

Dr. SAMORE. Senator, I was saying before you came in that I think the primary purpose of Iran's nuclear program is really strategic, I mean, to develop a military capacity under the guise of a nuclear power program.

Senator MARKEY. Well, how do we use this in our negotiations? How do we use the fact that they do not need nuclear-generated electricity? How do we use that in the negotiations given these realities?

Dr. SAMORE. Yes. I think it is hopeless to expect that we can persuade them to give up nuclear energy. What we are trying to achieve in these negotiations is to limit how they exercise their nuclear energy program, and in particular, we want to constrain——

Senator MARKEY. But we begin, in other words, with the premise that they do not need it. Okay? When they say nuclear power for electricity, we would not be building nuclear—we do not build nuclear power plants in America where natural gas is now so cheap. Right? That is why we got to keep the natural gas here, and we have got to keep the price low because it is backing out coal and backing out others.

Mr. Doran.

Dr. DORAN. Thanks. I completely agree with what you say. One of the more disturbing aspects of the way the administration has played its hand is it has created the sense that we are on the verge of an agreement with Iran, created the sense that the Iranians are really changing strategic direction, and as Senator Menendez suggested, creating the impression that it is intransigent elements in the United States and allies of the United States such as Saudi Arabia and Israel that are the real impediment. Instead of putting together our own coalition and taking a very reasonable position, making it clear to the world, we have created an impression out there that we are fighting against elements on our own side, which is really just bad negotiating.

Senator MARKEY. I will ask you a different question, Mr. Albright. We already have tight sanctions on Iran for their oil exports. They have got to keep a lot of their oil inside the country, and that which they can sell is limited. Now, the price of that which they can sell has now dropped from $110 a barrel down to $70 a barrel. So on top of the already tight sanctions, we have this additional reduction in revenues that is now going into a government dependent for 80 percent of its revenues on oil revenues. So what role is that going to play in these negotiations? How does that affect how they view what additional sanctions might be put on them or even this additional tightening which is occurring because of the collapse of the price of oil with no prospect for it going up in the near term?

Mr. ALBRIGHT. I think the decreasing oil prices are certainly going to be more pressure on Iran to make a deal. Whether it is enough——

Senator MARKEY. How big of a deal is this, though, this collapse of the energy price, given that we are having them keep millions of barrels of oil off the market as part of these sanctions? So what does it mean that the oil we let them sell has collapsed in price? It is down 40 percent. So what is that going to mean in terms of their negotiating posture in your view, given the pressure that is going to build internally?

Mr. ALBRIGHT. I think it is going to be—for the U.S. side, it is a development that is certainly going to incentivize Iran to make concessions. Whether it is enough—and it is also is Iran going to calculate, well, in a year from now, the prices will go up and we will get through it. I mean, that is part of this.

Senator MARKEY. In other words, are they immune domestically to this collapse in the price of oil, given the very educated population which they have? Can they ride that out for 2 or 3 years and have revenues just collapse in terms of the role that it is playing in the running of the government?

Mr. ALBRIGHT. I am not an Iranian expert. So I would say that, yes, they can. I mean, if they really do not want to deal, they can control their population——

Senator MARKEY. Mr. Samore, you seem to have a view on that.

Dr. SAMORE. Since 2009 when they put down a popular protest against the rigged elections that brought President Ahmadinejad to power, I think the government has been very effective in neutralizing political opposition. So again, I am not an Iran expert, but I agree with David that they are probably in pretty good shape to continue to ride out these economic difficulties.

Senator MARKEY. Can I say this? I believe that Putin and the Iranians are going to come under a lot of pressure. People might like Putin for what he is doing in the Ukraine. When that price of oil is down for a year or 2, I think you are going to see a big change in public opinion.

Can I ask one final, Mr. Chairman?

The CHAIRMAN.CHAIRMAN. Of course.

Senator MARKEY. Thank you.

I continue to be interested in the illicit procurement of materials made possible by Iran. I have asked the administration officials about this too. As a matter of fact, in a report this past June, the U.N. reminded us that Iran continues to maintain wide-reaching, transnational illicit procurement networks. It uses front companies to obtain materials on the global market for its nuclear and missile programs under the guise of legitimate commerce. These are complex operations, and they violate existing U.N. Security Council Resolution 1737.

Where can we tighten controls on the global market to thwart efforts by Iran and other likeminded countries to evade sanctions and acquire materials for its nuclear and missile programs?

Mr. ALBRIGHT. One immediate one is it is a vital part of the negotiations with Iran, that they commit not to continue doing illicit nuclear procurements. And that is one of the driving reasons to keep the U.N. Security Council sanctions on proliferation-sensitive goods in place. You could create an exemption for authorized nuclear programs. Like one was created for the Bushehr reactor. But the sanctions stay in place because you cannot have any confidence in being able to prevent a covert centrifuge plant if you cannot get control over their illicit procurements. They are going to have to buy a lot of things overseas in order to build such a facility. And so it is an urgent priority.

Beyond that, it is also very important to put pressure on China. Iran gets the dual-use goods—they could be made in America; they could be made in Germany—via China. So it is critical to increase pressure on China to enforce the sanctions and its own laws.

Senator MARKEY. The chairman has been very generous to me. Would you like to say a word, Mr. Doran?

Dr. DORAN. Yes, just quickly. That is one example of the importance of the possible military dimensions of them coming clean because it is not to have them say mea culpa, we were going for a bomb. It is to give us purview onto the procurement networks that they have, among other things.

Senator MARKEY. And Iran historically has had one of the highest prevarication coefficients of any country in the world when it deals with any of these nuclear or missile programs. And we just have to know that in dealing with them in any of these negotiations.

I thank you, Mr. Chairman.

The CHAIRMAN. Thank you.

You have been very gracious with your time, and I appreciate it. This is an incredibly important panel. You have a lot of expertise both on the scientific elements, as well as policy elements.

I do want to explore with Dr. Samore some of the lines of questions on the question of the role of Congress in sanctions. What is wrong with—not new sanctions. See that phrase ''new sanctions'' suggests we are going immediately to a whole new set of things we have not done, number one. But with calibrated, prospective sanctions that would be imposed, for example, possibly at the end of March if there is no framework that has been agreed to, that would say, you know what, you have no framework agreed to at the end of March, well, then we are going to go back to maybe the oil elements that we have basically told countries you do not have to meet the further reduced levels. We are going to back to that and/ or saying, you know, the amounts of money you are getting in relief—that is either going to be eliminated or cut in half or something like that, something that makes them understand that there are consequences for not coming to the conclusions that are necessary to actually make a deal that the international community could support and signaling to them that this is not an endless rolling negotiation which you can just game but something that you have to come to grips with in terms of your own answers. You may answer no at the end of the day because you think that regime preservation, you know, hegemonic goals and whatnot are more important. That is fine. But the world should know that at that point in time.

Dr. SAMORE. Well, it is a very good question.

I think the issue is whether that would be effective. And my concern is that some in Iran might actually welcome such legislation because they could very well calculate that will put more pressure on the P5+1 to make additional concessions in order to get a deal and avoid having the old sanctions imposed and then going back to the previous situation. Or the Iranians might calculate that if they stand pat and we impose those sanctions, it gives them a good reason to back away from the negotiations, blame the United States, and make it more difficult for us to build the coalition to resume sanctions. So I can understand why the administration has a lot of questions and concern about whether that kind of approach is going to be effective or whether it would actually boomerang and play into Iran's hands.

The CHAIRMAN. Let me go back to a question I put to you before, and I will open this to anybody on the panel, if the Ayatollah has always had the view that the regime is preserved by obtaining nuclear weapons, that the Islamic revolution in Iran is preserved by having nuclear weapons, that its hegemonic goals are preserved by having nuclear weapons, and he is the guy who has the ultimate decision, not Rouhani and Zarif, who we have aspirations for, but he is the guy who has the decision, then if you do nothing—nothing—beyond where you are at right now, how does that calculus ever change? It does not. You know, after 40 years of public service and negotiating as a school board trustee, a mayor, a State legislator, 22 years in Congress, I have never seen that something stays the same unless some dynamic element is introduced that changes the equation. And if everything stays the same, then how is it that you change the equation for the Ayatollah?

Dr. SAMORE. I have tried to suggest some things that we could do, both the United States and our allies, to try to change that calculation. One, as I think all of us have said, is that we have put enough reasonable ideas on the table. It is now time for Iran to show that they are actually prepared to move toward us. And my sense is that the negotiations broke up in Vienna with the ball very clearly in Zarif's court. So let us see whether he can get some additional flexibility from the Supreme Leader. I am skeptical but I am willing to wait and see whether or not.

Secondly, as I said, we need to make the threat of additional sanctions very credible and tangible to the Iranians by visibly working with our allies to prepare for further reductions in Iranian oil exports.

And third, I hope that there is some way that Congress and the White House could work together positively to come up with legislation that makes the threat of additional sanctions more credible for the Iranians.

But, you know, look, I agree with you, Senator, that it may very well be that nothing we do will convince Khamenei to fundamentally change his position. I think that is quite likely. And in that case, we are talking about how do we put ourselves in the best position after the collapse of the Joint Plan of Action to increase the sanctions.

Mr. ALBRIGHT. I actually would strongly endorse what Gary said, that there is a need for Congress and the administration to work together, because ultimately it is as simple as coming up with a plan B. If you think the deal is going to fall apart, you do not want to start your planning the day it falls apart. And so I think there is a critical need to think these things through now, and I think Congress has an essential role to play in that, particularly as the world recognizes they are the ones who came up with the sanctions that have gotten Iran to the negotiating table.

I also think that the administration has gotten itself into some perplexing boxes. The PMD issue is one to me where if you, in a sense, throw the IAEA under the bus by deferring the PMD in a sense indefinitely, you have just weakened the credibility and the ability of the verification entity to verify the very deal that they are negotiating. And you are creating precedents. Yes, it is okay, Iran. You do not have to let the IAEA go to military sites. Yes, you do not have to let them have access to experts that were involved in these alleged covert activities. So you are jeopardizing the very verifiability of the agreement. And so I think there is the need for action to break the administration out of these—I do not know what to call it—a dueler well. That is a very old term from computer days. They are just caught spinning around and around.

And I would argue that the sanctions issue in the debate between Congress and the administration is another one, that it has been reduced to rhetoric and threats. And yet, there is an incredibly important role that both play in creating the threat of sanctions.

The CHAIRMAN. Yes. I agree with you. I do not disagree from my perspective. I speak only for myself. Personally I am more than willing to work with the administration. As a matter of fact, we have done that in the past. The problem is that what you hear from the administration at this point is do not worry about that. The Iranians know that if it does not move forward, there will be more sanctions coming, that Congress will be happy to do that. I do not think that that is real enough, crystallized enough for the Iranians, or tangible enough to know, well, what is it that is coming because if I am in the midst of, let us say, an election, I want to have a pretty good idea of what is coming, and I will calculate based upon that of what I will have to do. Oh, there will be more sanctions. Well, how severe? Is it only what I was able to survive? Is it more significant than that? You know, I think that just the waiting and suggesting that, well, when and if we get there, they know that the Congress is more than willing to pursue sanctions has no real meaningfulness to it.

And I think that the other part—and I may be wrong about this, but my sense is that the Iranians have a view that there is no credible military threat on the table at least at this point, that maybe there will be at some point in the future if they move forward. But I do not think that they feel that there is a present credible military threat which in the back of their mind would have to be a consequence. Maybe you are right, Dr. Samore, that if it all breaks down and they start moving rapidly forward, that the West, either the United States and whoever else, might strike them. But right now, they do not believe there is a credible military threat.

And right now, my perspective is that they do not really believe that we are going to reimpose any sanctions or produce any new sanctions because what they see is the administration fending off, which is a different signal than I think what you are talking about, saying, no, do not do anything. Just stay out of our way. Versus, well, let us do something and let them know that in fact there are some real consequences here. And it is that dynamic that is, I think, inopportune in terms of strengthening our hands in the negotiations at the end of the day.

Dr. SAMORE. Can I say, sir, I think that it is clear that if the talks fail and the JPOA collapses, the Iranians and others will try to blame Congress as being the main culprit here? And I think it is very important that we take steps that take that argument away from them. And so that is why I think—I completely agree with you—that an approach between the administration and Congress that defines and specifies the magnitude of the sanctions and yet leaves enough discretion so that the administration can accept it is the most effective way to show that we are acting in a united way and really deny the Iranians the ability to blame Congress for blowing up these negotiations.

The CHAIRMAN. I am sure they blame us for putting them in a position that already puts them at the negotiations.

And I heard so often—I have to be honest with you, which is one of my own personal senses of calibrating this. Unfortunately, at every turn that the Congress led on the question of sanctions, administration witnesses consistently came before this committee and said that would be a grave mistake, that that would break apart the comity that we had with the European Union and with other allies, that it would be a, disaster. Well, I have to be honest with you. Those apocalyptic views never ultimately materialized, and if anything, it was the congressional insistence that got us to the point where the Iranians felt compelled to be at the table.

So I think that is part of the equation here as well. When you get stiff-armed and you are told that in fact your view at the end of the day, which history—at least short-term history—has proven to be that we were right and others who took that view were wrong, that moving forward, you would hope that there would be a more constructive role to embrace the opportunity to strengthen the hand of negotiators at the end of the day. I just do not think that that is there.

Senator Corker.

Senator CORKER. Thank you.

Dr. Samore, you threw out the notion that if we were to pass sanctions that would kick in in the event that a deal was not reached, it could hasten our side to make a bad deal. Now, is that something you just threw out or is that something that has been discussed, that some of our partners, if you will, who are negotiating are concerned that if Congress acted in that manner, it could in fact—while we have some allies who already think we have over-given, it might prompt them to do even more. Is that something you just threw out at this meeting, or has that been discussed by others?

Dr. SAMORE. No one has expressed that concern to me. But what I worry about is that is how the Iranians will see it, whether it is true or not, and that might make them even more intransigent because, you know, look, if the Iranians have a pessimistic view about the outcome of these negotiations, which is what the Supreme Leader says over and over again publicly—he says I do not mind if these negotiations go out, but I do not think they will succeed because I do not think the Americans will accept our nuclear program. And I agree with him. We are not going to accept their nuclear program. So if both sides anticipate the very likelihood that the talks will collapse, and they will fail, and the Joint Plan of Action will fall apart, then both sides are going to be maneuvering in order to cast as much blame as possible on the other side. And what I worry is that the Iranians may think that if they are patient and they just keep the talks going with little concessions here and there, sooner or later, Congress will take steps that will end the talks over the President's objection, and it will give them a greater ability to avoid additional sanctions once the process ends.

Senator CORKER. From the other groups that we are associated with.

Mr. ALBRIGHT. I think the concern—this has been discussed. I think Gary would agree, I guess I will call them trigger sanctions that come into effect in a mandatory way, he would agree that that is perceived by the Iranians as putting a gun to their head. That leads them to put together what I would call trigger advancements in their nuclear program. They did this last December and January; the parliament said they would pass a law that required Iran to produce 60 percent enriched uranium if new sanctions were imposed. So there is worry about that, that the trigger sanctions could backfire.

And then there is also the worry that in that environment the Iranians would start resisting in the negotiations. And so I think that that is a concern that has to be addressed.

I think what I am talking about, though, is sanctions discussions and plans that are not necessarily required to take effect but would give the President the authority to use those sanctions at least through this period where there is uncertainty about the future of the JPA.

Senator CORKER. Of course, he has a lot of leeway in that regard without us doing that. So I understand it is a tilt. But again, he can put a lot of sanctions in place without us being involved in any way.

Let me ask you this. What would be your perceived response, without having a great deal of time to think about it, if we pass legislation that said that the implementation of this agreement could not be—the money would be withdrawn to implement it unless Congress approved it? So we are not saying what sanctions would be put in place down the road, but we are saying that unless Congress approves this deal, it cannot be implemented. What do you think the impact would be on the negotiations if something like that were to pass both the House and Senate?

Mr. ALBRIGHT. I think it would be negative on the Iranian side because they already do not trust the United States to take away the sanctions.

But I must say I am torn because I think more congressional oversight on this problem is urgent. We are struggling to know what is even being discussed and you are Members of Congress. So I think the oversight is necessary, and whether it is the Congress approving or the Senate approving the deal or not, I think that something has to happen.

And I think this is a mistake the administration is making. I did work a lot on first opposing the agreed framework and then being convinced to support it. The fact that the Congress was not on board was a severely corrosive factor. And so I think it is important the administration work with Congress to make sure this is a united effort and a deal that is supported.

Dr. SAMORE. I just want to say I think one of the big obstacles to the White House and Congress reaching agreement on language of legislation is what would exactly constitute an acceptable deal because right now my sense from letters from Congress and legislation and so forth it is setting out terms and conditions for an agreement which the administration does not think they can achieve through this negotiation. And without saying who is right or who is wrong, I think as long as there is such a divergence in terms of what would constitute an acceptable deal, I think it is difficult to come to an agreement on whether Congress should put itself in the position of approving an agreement.

Of course, the fact is if the administration comes forward with a bad deal that accepts anything close to having Iran with a significant enrichment capability, I would expect Congress to overrule that deal. I mean, Congress would pass legislation that would make it impossible for the President to waive sanctions. And I think that is a real constraint on what the administration thinks it has to negotiate in order to pass political muster in this town.

Senator CORKER. But having it put in place in advance of completing negotiations that Congress had to approve the deal you believe would have a negative effect on negotiations.

Dr. SAMORE. I am not sure if it would have a negative effect on negotiations, but I think the administration would be reluctant to accept such legislation when there is such a divergence between what they think a deal is going to look like and what Congress has expressed as the essential elements of a deal, including all the things we are talking about, that there be a dismantlement of Iran's illicit nuclear program, the question of a possible military dimension has to be resolved in its entirety. I mean, those are not things that are likely to be in the deal that is currently being negotiated.

Senator CORKER. I would say from their perspective, though, then people in the Senate and House would be firing with real bullets as far as whether they approved the deal or not. And I would say that while people can be bellicose and sometimes over the top, that people sitting there and actually deciding yea or nay whether this whole thing falls apart could cause people—looking at it from the administration's perspective if they wanted to actually view Congress this way, could cause people to be more responsible than they think. Do you understand what I am saying? From their perspective. I think responsible is getting a deal that does not lead to them having nuclear capabilities, but I do not think it would go just in one direction.

Let me just ask one last question. What are the economic drivers that—over time people worry about this sanctions regime falling apart. What are the biggest elements that are driving some of the other countries to want to go ahead and let this dissipate so they can continue to do business? Is it the oil itself that comes from Iran? Is that the biggest driver? What do you think is the biggest issue for China and Russia and some of the other countries?

Dr. SAMORE. Well, I think it is both oil but also it is the Iranian market. I mean, when the Joint Plan of Action was originally agreed, there was a real question about whether limited sanctions relief would lead to a much broader erosion of the sanctions that are in place. And the Iranians certainly tried as hard as they could to lure companies to Tehran and offer them all kinds of deals. And so far, I think to the credit of the United States and its allies, the governments have been able to restrain companies from breaking the remaining sanctions, including limits on oil purchases, with the one exception of China where we have seen some important slippage especially in purchases of condensate. And I think that is an important issue for the administration to demonstrate that it can get China back in the box. But the other big oil customers have all continued to keep their purchases from Iran at the levels they were at when the Joint Plan of Action went into effect.

So we have been able to demonstrate so far that the Joint Plan of Action has not eroded the overall regime. And of course, the Iranians will keep trying and companies will still be tempted, and we will have to continue to jawbone and apply sanctions in order to make sure that that does not happen.

Senator CORKER. And I will stop with this. I know the chairman needs to go and I do too. You all do too.

We have companies here in our own Nation that would love to export condensate—right—and are prohibited from doing that today. Just on that element, condensate, let us face it, is a byproduct of exploration. We wish it would have been part of more closely—you know, we did not pay enough attention—our Nation did—when we were negotiating the deal with Iran in the first place. But what if we supplanted that condensate need for countries like China and other places? Would that have an effect on us being able to keep the regime together?

Dr. SAMORE. I am strongly in favor of the United States exporting energy to not only China but also our Asian allies. If we are asking countries to shift their purchases, even if there are other oil and other products from the Saudis and others, I think it is very important that the U.S. export its energy, both oil and gas.

Senator CORKER. Thank you.

The CHAIRMAN. Can you direct exports? It is a global market. Can we take and say we are going to only want these to be sold to our allies, whether they be Asia or anybody else?

Dr. SAMORE. Well, I mean, my understanding from talking to people who have recently been in China, also Korea and Japan is that they would love to buy more energy from the United States because they see it not only as price competitive but also a much more secure and reliable source than most of the Middle East countries. So I think the market would take care of it if we made it available.

The CHAIRMAN. You think the market would take care of it, that it would not go just to the highest bidder. You mean the businesses would now move to a different philosophy of what is the very essentials of the economics debut, which is they extract, do the processing, that cost them X number of dollars. And normally they want to go and sell it to the highest in the marketplace.

Dr. SAMORE. I think U.S. companies would be able to sell at a profit U.S. energy resources to Asia, yes.

The CHAIRMAN. Yes, but would that be the highest marketplace? What if China is willing to pay $10 per barrel more than Japan or South Korea? Do you really think that the energy companies will say, well, we are going to forego the extra $10 per barrel to sell it to Japan and South Korea?

Dr. SAMORE. No, I do not expect them to do that. But if there is a price bidding process, then I think the Japanese and the Koreans might look to match the Chinese price.

The CHAIRMAN. Under those circumstances, yes, I could see it.

But this is part of the problem. I do not know. Maybe if you extract it from Federal lands or waters, you could put a condition that it has to be sold to certain allies, certain regions. But that is one of my concerns about—I do not have an ideological opposition to using energy as long as you can use selling domestic energy internationally, but the question is in an international market, it goes to the highest bidder. That is our big challenge. So how does one direct it for your strategic purposes at the end of the day, whether that be Asia or Ukraine, for example?

Dr. SAMORE. Well, of course, we do have a very large strategic petroleum reserve, and I think that I would be in favor of using that for foreign policy purposes. I cannot say whether this is the right one, but I think we should think about using——

The CHAIRMAN. That is a little different than just commercial extraction.

One last thing. I am exploring your idea. I am not in opposition to it. I am trying to figure out how you get to where you want to be.

Go ahead.

Senator CORKER. Well, if I could, just on this one issue of condensate. It is my understanding—and I could be way off base—that the way this actually works is that they enter into long-term contracts for the delivery between companies and China. And I think it is not quite like the petroleum market as it relates to this. It is a little different in that this is used in petrochemicals and other kinds of development. And I think there maybe is a little bit better way of having an impact on China in this particular regard than maybe with some of the other things we talked about with LNG and others.

The CHAIRMAN. If we are talking only about condensates, Commerce has allowed some condensates to be sold, and they seem to be pretty reluctant towards limiting any further condensates. See, I thought we were talking about much more than condensates. But in any event, I am sure that the soon-to-be chairman is going to explore that as we move forward.

Thank you all for your testimony and incredible sharing of time. As you can see, there is a real interest by the ranking member and myself, as well as other members, to go to the depth of trying to understand the dynamics here.

My final comment is—well, one is that this record will remain open until the close of business on Friday.

And secondly is this is a traditional challenge between the role of the executive branch and the legislative branch. I am sure the executive branch would never want the legislative branch to necessarily involve themselves with authorizations of use of military force. Some of us believe that that is an appropriate and needed action by the Congress when we are engaging our sons and daughters to be sent abroad. And by the same token, on this question it was Congress' failure to get engaged that led us end up having to face the challenges of a nuclear-armed North Korea. So there is a balance here at the end of the day, and we have got to figure out how we get that balance right for what I do believe is our collective vision of not having Iran have nuclear weapons but about how that is frameworked in a way that makes it less likely than more likely is a concern many of us.

But with the thanks of the committee for all of your insights, this hearing is now adjourned.

[Whereupon, at 4:20 p.m., the hearing was adjourned.]

―――――――――

ADDITIONAL MATERIAL SUBMITTED FOR THE RECORD

GRAPHS AND ANNEX SUBMITTED WITH DAVID ALBRIGHT'S PREPARED STATEMENT

Figure 1: Four Step Enrichment Predictions with no near 20 Percent LEU
Breakout Time Calculation (includes 2 week setup time)
4000, 6000, 10000, 14000, 18000 IR-1 Centrifuges
Range of 3.5% Inventory Used, 0-1000 kg UF$_6$

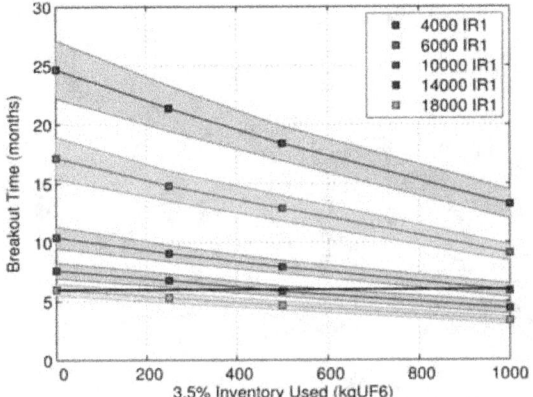

Mean (with range) breakout time versus 3.5% inventory used

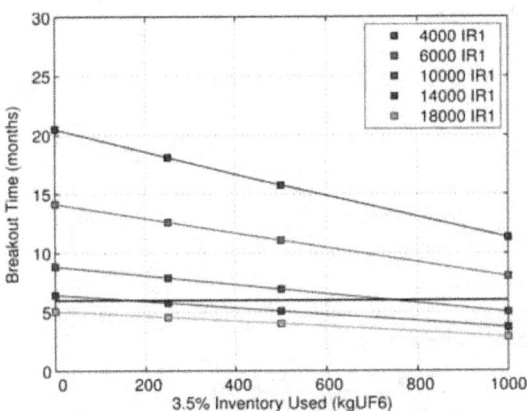

Minimum breakout time versus 3.5% inventory used.

Note: The results are calculated as breakout times for various numbers of centrifuges and amounts of 3.5% inventory used, with multiple scenarios for each number of centrifuges matched with a specific 3.5% inventory. Two sets of breakout times are reported in the figures mean with range and minimum value of all scenarios. The results in the text use the mean values. The minimum values are viewed as worst case estimates which may be unlikely to be achieved in practice.

Figure 2: Four Step Enrichment Estimate with 50 kg near 20 percent LEUF$_6$ Used
Breakout Time Calculation (includes 2 week setup time)
4000, 6000, 10000, 14000, 18000 IR-1 Centrifuges
Range of 3.5% Inventory Used: 0-1000 kg LEUF$_6$

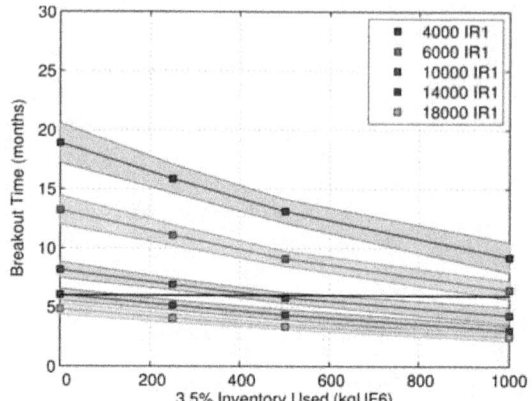

Mean (with range) breakout time versus 3.5% inventory used

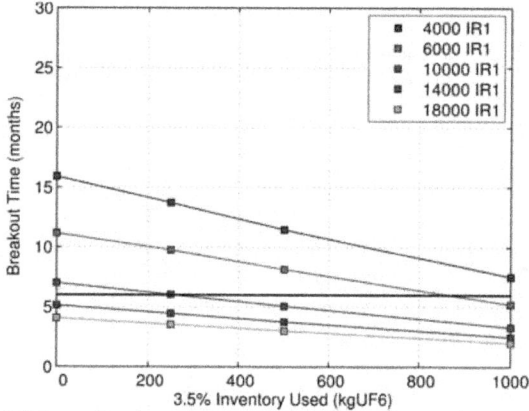

Minimum breakout time versus 3.5% inventory used

Note: The results are calculated as breakout times for various numbers of centrifuges and amounts of 3.5% inventory used, with multiple scenarios for each number of centrifuges matched with a specific 3.5% inventory. Two sets of breakout times are reported in the figures: mean with range and minimum value of all scenarios. The results in the text use the mean values. The minimum values are viewed as worst case estimates which may be unlikely to be achieved in practice.

ANNEX: PROVISIONS IN A LONG TERM, COMPREHENSIVE AGREEMENT

The negotiations for a long-term deal are highly detailed and secret. Many technical provisions are being studied and proposed by the P5+1 negotiators, particularly U.S. officials. Iran has resisted many of these proposals and rejected most proposals that would lead to significantly lengthened breakout times. It is unclear if the differences can be bridged over the next several months.

Nonetheless, it makes sense to review a set of provisions that can form the basis of a comprehensive solution able to protect adequately U.S. national security interests. This list has been developed based on a range of information and attempts to incorporate information about the provisions being discussed during the negotiations. However, there is no attempt to represent the U.S. or its allies' positions. For more detail about the provisions presented here, the reader is referred to the ISIS Web sites.

This list of provisions is an update from lists prepared by ISIS in December 2013 and January 2014. The changes from those early lists reflect known concessions made by the parties to the negotiations, new developments not foreseen a year ago, or efforts to seek compromises. In addition, many of the provisions work together, such as limiting the number of IR–1 centrifuges, leaving only a small number of advanced centrifuges, mandating significantly reduced stocks of LEU, and removing or destroying centrifuges and associated equipment. As such, while specific limits can be set individually as below, when key provisions are considered in their entirety, these provisions may each differ from the cases stated below. However, the goal of a one year breakout would still be obtained.

The provisions are organized in two broad categories, those without duration and those with a duration of 20 years. The latter could be subject to a phasing, such as after a fraction of the 20 years has passed, that would lead to gradual relaxation of the conditions or replacement by others. However, phasing is not included in this list.

CONDITIONS WITHOUT A DEFINED DURATION

- The Arak reactor complex will be modified to use enriched uranium fuel and a smaller core structure, or calandria. The reactor's power will be reduced from the level currently planned; i.e., 40 megawatts-thermal, and the reactor's heat removal system will be modified to fit that lower power rating.
- Iran will not reprocess any irradiated fuel or build a facility capable of reprocessing.
- Iran will not enrich above 5 percent in the isotope uranium 235, and will not produce stocks of enriched uranium that exceed in quantity the needs of its civilian program, noting that it has long term LEU fuel delivery agreements with Russia and would be expected to have additional ones with foreign reactor vendors after the conclusion of a comprehensive solution.
- Iran will commit not to procure goods for its nuclear programs abroad in a manner that is considered illicit ("illicit nuclear commodity trafficking or trade").

CONDITIONS AND PARAMETERS WITH A DEFINED DURATION OF 20 YEARS

- Iran will have only one enrichment site, the one at Natanz, and it will utilize IR–1 centrifuges. The number installed will be consistent with a one year breakout timeframe. Considering significant reductions in LEU stocks, the number of allowed centrifuges could reach 4,000–5,000 IR–1 centrifuges.
- The Fordow enrichment site will be shut down or converted into a non-centrifuge-related site.
- Centrifuge research and development will be limited to centrifuges equivalent to the IR–2m centrifuge. The number of centrifuge cascades will be limited in number, and no cascade will have more than a few tens of centrifuges. In all cases, the number of advanced centrifuges in a cascade would be far lower than the amount to be used in a production-scale cascade.
- Major centrifuge component manufacturing and storage locations will be limited in number and identified.
- Centrifuge assembly will occur only at the Natanz enrichment site.
- In the case of the IR–1 centrifuges, centrifuge manufacturing would be limited to the replacement of broken centrifuges, if no spares exist. For example, in the case of IR–1 centrifuges, a stock of many thousands of uninstalled centrifuges would be stored and then drawn upon to replace broken ones. Thus, Iran would agree not to build any IR–1 centrifuges until this stock is exhausted.[1]
- When the long-term agreement takes effect, centrifuges and all associated cascade equipment in excess of the cap would be turned off, so that no centrifuges are operating and the cascades are not under vacuum. Centrifuges would be turned off in a controlled manner so as to limit centrifuge damage. Excess centrifuges and the cascades containing them would be disabled in a manner so as to require 6 to 12 months to restart disabled cascades. Based on public information about the negotiations, excess centrifuges would not be destroyed but rather equipment from the cascades and centrifuges would be removed from the centrifuge plants making restart very time-consuming. To ensure adequate build-back times, certain centrifuge or cascade equipment would be selectively destroyed. Any storage of equipment or uninstalled centrifuges would be subject to rigorous IAEA monitoring.

- Iran will not build any conversion lines that can convert enriched uranium oxide into hexafluoride form.
- LEU stocks will be limited, based on a realistic civil justification.
    - Æ With regard to near 20 percent LEU, Iran will not possess any such LEU in hexafluoride form and its total stock in unirradiated oxide form, including in fresh fuel elements and assemblies and scrap and waste, will be less than the equivalent of 100 kg of near 20 percent LEU hexafluoride. During the life of the agreement, this unirradiated stock will be further reduced to below the equivalent of 50 kg of near 20 percent LEU hexafluoride.
    - Æ Iran will not possess more than the equivalent of 500 kilograms of unirradiated, less than 5 percent LEU hexafluoride. Iran's practical needs for LEU, such as in the modified Arak reactor, would require the use of a certain amount of LEU in a fuel fabrication pipeline. This amount would be determined as part of the agreement. Excess LEU will be shipped out of Iran.
- Uranium mining, milling, and conversion facilities will be limited in throughput to the actual need for enrichment or other mutually agreed upon use.
- Iran would ratify the Additional Protocol and accept a range of supplementary verification measures, including but not limited to,
    - Æ More detailed declarations of and greater access to uranium supplies and sources;
    - Æ Detailed declarations of the number of centrifuges made in total, its total used and accumulated stocks of raw materials and equipment needed to build and operate centrifuges.
- Prior to the relaxation of major economic or financial sanctions, Iran will address the IAEA's concerns about past and possibly ongoing nuclear weapons or nuclear weapons-related work.
- United Nations Security Council sanctions on proliferation sensitive goods will continue throughout the duration of the agreement. At the beginning of the period of the comprehensive solution, a verified procurement channel will be established for items needed in Iran's nuclear programs. The list of items will be established by mutual agreement and will include major nuclear facilities, nuclear components, nuclear and nuclear-related dual-use goods, and other sensitive items such as those on watch lists. Procurements of listed items outside this channel will be banned and considered illicit nuclear trade.
- Iran will not export or otherwise transfer nuclear materials, reactors, centrifuges, reprocessing equipment, other nuclear facilities or equipment, or the means to make such equipment or facilities to any state, company, or other entity.[2]
- By the end of the period in which the comprehensive solution will be in force, Iran will implement an export control system in line with the requirements of the four main export control regimes (lists and guidance) and submit a comprehensive report to the 1540 Committee on Iran's implementation of the resolution. Iran will also commit not to export or otherwise transfer reprocessing or enrichment technologies or goods to any state or non-state actor after the comprehensive solution period ends.

Notes

[1] Broken centrifuges will be replaced with centrifuges of the same type. This should mean, for example, that an installed IR–1 centrifuge would be replaced with an IR–1 centrifuge of the same design and enrichment capability as the one removed. A broken centrifuge is defined as one that has a rotor assembly incapable of spinning under power and cannot be repaired.

[2] A model condition developed by ISIS: The state of concern agrees not to transfer to any state or entity whatsoever, or in any way help a state or entity obtain, nuclear weapons or explosive devices, or components of such weapons; nuclear material; nuclear know-how or technology; or equipment, material, goods, technology designed for, prepared for, or that can contribute to the processing, use, or production of nuclear materials for nuclear weapons or in sanctioned nuclear programs.